SUPER EASY

KETO

Mediterranean Diet

Cookbook for Seniors

2000+ Days Simple and Delicious Recipes for your Everyday Healthy Living Meal Plan.

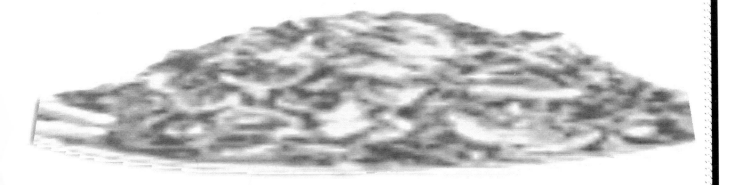

Loretta Dudley

Disclaimer

The information provided in "Super Easy Keto Mediterranean Diet Cookbook for Seniors" is for educational and informational purposes only and is not intended as medical advice. Always consult with your healthcare provider before making any dietary changes, particularly if you have any pre-existing health conditions or concerns. The author and publisher are not responsible for any adverse effects or consequences resulting from the use of any recipes or suggestions herein. Individual results may vary.

Gratitude Page

Thank you for selecting the "Super Easy Keto Mediterranean Diet Cookbook for Seniors" Your road to a healthier, more vibrant life demonstrates your devotion and commitment to well-being. It is an honor to be a part of that journey, and I am really grateful for the opportunity to share this collection of recipes and insights with you.

This book is the result of love, care, and many hours of research and testing. My greatest gratitude goes out to my beloved grandma, Margaret, whose health problems and subsequent rehabilitation inspired every page of this book. Her resiliency and zest for life serve as the foundation for these recipes.

I am also grateful to my family and friends, who have supported and encouraged me throughout my quest. Your suggestions, taste tests, and persistent belief in the importance of this work have been helpful.

Thanks to the health professionals and nutrition experts who provided advise and shared their knowledge. Your expertise helped shape the nutritional content and practical **recommendations in this book.**

Finally, to the reader: Thank you for putting your trust in this cookbook. Your health and well-being are extremely important, and I sincerely hope that the recipes and tips on these pages bring you joy, sustenance, and vigor.

I invite you to share your experiences, ideas, and suggestions. Your feedback is not only appreciated, but also required to continuously improve and enrich future editions of this work. Together, we can establish a resource that will help many more people on their path to better health.

I wish you a trip filled with tasty meals, excellent health, and happiness.

How to use this book

Welcome to the "Keto Mediterranean Diet Cookbook for Seniors: Tested and Trusted Low-Carb Recipes for Weight Loss and Heart-Healthy Aging with Picture Guide." This cookbook is designed to be your comprehensive guide to embracing a nutritious and enjoyable lifestyle through the fusion of the ketogenic and Mediterranean diets. xxzHere's how to make the most of the wealth of information and recipes contained within these pages:

1. Understanding the Basics

Start with the foundational chapters to grasp the core principles of the keto and Mediterranean diets. In the "Overview of the Ketogenic and Mediterranean Diets," you'll learn about the benefits and scientific basis of each dietary approach. This section sets the stage for why combining these diets can be particularly beneficial for seniors.

2. Discovering the Benefits for Seniors

Open the chapter on "Benefits of Combining Both Approaches for Seniors." This section highlights how this hybrid diet can address specific health concerns common in older adults, such as heart health, weight management, and cognitive function. Understanding these benefits will motivate you to integrate the dietary principles into your daily life.

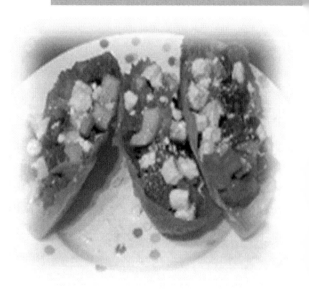

3. Practical Guidance and Meal Planning

Navigate through chapters like "Nutritional Requirements for Healthy Aging in Your Golden Years" and "How the Keto Mediterranean Diet Addresses Senior Health Needs." These chapters provide detailed insights into the essential nutrients required for optimal health and how this diet meets those needs.

4. Essential Kitchen Equipment and Ingredients

Before you start cooking, make sure you have everything you need. The chapters "Must-Have Kitchen Equipment for Seniors" and "Key Ingredients for a Keto Mediterranean Pantry" offer practical advice on equipping your kitchen with tools and ingredients that make meal preparation straightforward and enjoyable.

5. Shopping and Budgeting Tips

Shopping Tips and Ingredient Substitutions for Seniors on a Budget" provides valuable advice on how to make healthy eating affordable. Learn how to shop smart, make the best use of seasonal produce, and substitute ingredients without compromising on flavor or nutrition.

6. Meal Planning and Prep

In "Simple Meal Planning Techniques for Seniors" and "Weekly Meal Prep Tips to Save Time and Energy," you'll find strategies to streamline your cooking process. These chapters help you organize your meals efficiently, ensuring you always have healthy options available.

7. Recipes for Every Occasion

The heart of this book lies in its recipes, categorized for convenience:

- ✓ **Breakfasts:** Start your day with energy-boosting options detailed in "7 Days of Energizing Keto Mediterranean Breakfast Recipes for Seniors."
- ✓ **Lunches**: Enjoy mid-day meals that sustain and nourish you with recipes from "7 Days of Nourishing Keto Mediterranean Lunch Recipes for Seniors."
- ✓ **Dinners:** Savor hearty and nutritious dinners from "7 Days of Flavorful Keto Mediterranean Dinner Recipes That Don't Compromise on Nutrition for Seniors."
- ✓ **Snacks:** Keep your energy up with "7 Days of Wholesome Keto Mediterranean Snack Ideas for Midday Boosts for Seniors."
- ✓ **Side Dishes:** Complement your main meals with vibrant side dishes from "7 Days of Vibrant Keto Mediterranean Side Dish Recipes Featuring Fresh Produce for Seniors."
- ✓ **Desserts:** Indulge your sweet tooth healthily with "7 Days of Guilt-Free Keto Mediterranean Dessert Recipes for Sweet Tooth Satisfaction for Seniors."
- ✓ **Festive Recipes:** Celebrate special occasions with "7 Days of Easy Keto Mediterranean Festive Recipes to Celebrate Holidays and Special Occasions for Seniors."

Each recipe includes detailed nutritional information, prep time, ingredients, and step-by-step instructions to ensure your cooking experience is as smooth and enjoyable as possible.

8. Health and Wellness Guidance

For a holistic approach to health, refer to chapters like "Importance of Physical Activity for Senior Health" and "Incorporating Morning and Evening Exercise to Enhance Your Progress." These sections emphasize the role of physical activity in complementing your dietary efforts.

9. Holistic Wellness

The chapter on "Holistic Approaches to Wellness and Aging Gracefully" offers insights into incorporating mindfulness, stress management, and self-care practices into your daily routine. These tips help you achieve overall well-being beyond diet and exercise.

10. Stay Engaged and Connected

Use the practical ideas and tips in this book to stay active and make the most of your golden years. The conclusion invites you to share your experiences and feedback, allowing others to benefit from your journey and contribute to the ongoing growth of this resource.

By following the advice and recipes in this book, you will be able to make informed decisions that improve your health, vitality, and overall quality of life. Enjoy the wonderful meals, embrace the holistic wellness techniques, and live your golden years with confidence and joy.

TABLE OF CONTENT

INRODUCTION

I'm Loretta Dudley, and I'm excited to take you on a culinary trip that combines the best of two robust diets: the ketogenic and Mediterranean. This book is specifically designed for seniors who want to improve their health, maintain a healthy weight, and eat tasty, nutritious foods.

Allow me to share a personal story with you. My grandmother, a bright woman who suffered a variety of health issues in her final years, inspired me to write this book. During her trip, we noticed that combining the ketogenic and Mediterranean diet concepts improved her health and well-being significantly. The recipes in this book have been tried and true, and they were inspired by my grandmother's desire for nutritional, heart-healthy meals without sacrificing flavor. Her great response to these meals inspired me to gather them for you, in the hopes of bringing the same advantages to your table.

This book includes more than just recipes. It provides:

✓ Detailed Guidance: From understanding the basics of the ketogenic and Mediterranean diets to practical tips on meal planning, shopping, and preparing delicious meals.

✓ Health-Focused Recipes: Every recipe is designed with seniors in mind, focusing on low-carb, heart-healthy, and easy-to-make dishes.

✓ Holistic Wellness Tips: Beyond diet, this book includes advice on physical activity, mindfulness, and overall well-being to support a balanced lifestyle.

✓ Visual Guide: With picture guides for each recipe, you'll find it easy to follow along and create beautiful, nutritious meals.

This book is specifically targeted at seniors who are keen on improving their health through diet. Whether you're looking to manage your weight, enhance your heart health, or simply enjoy more nutritious meals, this cookbook is for you. The recipes and tips provided are tailored to meet the unique nutritional needs and preferences of older adults, making healthy eating both accessible and enjoyable.

I know you will enjoy this book, and I will like to invite you to explore my other works that offer additional pathways to health and wellness:

DASH Diet Mediterranean Weight Loss Solution: This book blends the principles of the DASH and Mediterranean diets, focusing on sustainable weight loss and heart health. It's a perfect companion to further your journey towards a healthier lifestyle.

Sugar Elimination lDiet Cookbook for Beginners: This book is designed to help you reduce sugar intake effectively, with beginner-friendly recipes and tips to support your journey to better health.

These books provide different yet complementary approaches to healthy living, offering a variety of recipes and strategies to help you achieve your health goals.

To get these books are very simple, just follow the easy steps in the next page:

Kindly bring out your phone and:

1. Locate the QR of the required book

2. Open your smartphone QR scanner

3. Wait a little, notification will appear on your screen with a link or prompt

4. Tap the notification or link that appears

5. Follow the on-screen instruction to navigate

For more book like this:

Your journey with me will help you discover how easy and enjoyable healthy eating can be. These recipes have brought joy and health to my family, and I hope they do the same for you. Your feedback is invaluable, so please share your experiences and thoughts. It helps me improve and guide others who are seeking to make positive changes in their lives.

Thank you for allowing me to be a part of your journey to better health. Let's cook, eat, and thrive together.

Chapter One

Overview of the Ketogenic and Mediterranean Diets

Hello, and welcome to the Keto Mediterranean Diet. Today, we'll explore the keto Mediterranean diet. It's all about eating great, nutritious foods. Prepare to feel wonderful and enjoy delicious meals!

The Keto Mediterranean Diet combines two well-known nutritional approaches to aid weight loss, heart health, and overall well-being, making it ideal for seniors. This book explores the Ketogenic and Mediterranean diets, including their concepts, benefits, and practical applications. Diets, providing you with a full understanding as you embark on your road toward healthier eating habits..

Let's start with the Ketogenic Diet, a low-carbohydrate, high-fat diet that has grown in popularity due to its potential to induce ketosis, a metabolic state in which the body burns fat for fuel. The Ketogenic Diet emphasizes healthy fats, moderate protein intake, and low carbohydrates, which generally consist of fewer than 50 grams of net carbs per day.

The Ketogenic Diet for seniors, offers numerous potential benefits, including weight loss, improved blood sugar control, enhanced cognitive function, and increased energy levels. By restricting carbohydrates and increasing fat intake, the Ketogenic Diet helps stabilize blood sugar levels, reduce inflammation, and promote satiety, making it an ideal choice for managing weight and supporting overall health.

Now, Let's look at the Mediterranean Diet, which is based on the historic eating patterns of Mediterranean nations.

The Mediterranean Diet focuses on full, unprocessed foods such fruits, vegetables, whole grains, legumes, nuts, seeds, fish, and olive oil, while limiting intake of red meat, processed foods, and sugar.

The Mediterranean Diet is known for its multiple health benefits, including a lower risk of heart disease, stroke, cancer, and cognitive decline. The Mediterranean Diet provides seniors with a plethora of nutrients, antioxidants, and anti-inflammatory chemicals that promote heart health, cognitive function, and overall lifespan.

The Mediterranean Diet prioritizes plant-based foods, healthy fats, and lean protein sources, resulting in a balanced and sustainable eating plan that supports health and well-being long into your senior years.

Now that we've discussed the separate benefits of the Ketogenic and Mediterranean Diets, let's look at the synergistic advantages of combining these two dietary methods to form the Keto Mediterranean Diet. The Keto Mediterranean Diet, which incorporates parts of both diets, provides a unique combination of low-carbohydrate, high-fat, and nutrient-dense meals that support weight reduction, heart health, and good aging in seniors.

The Keto Mediterranean Diet focuses on quality and sustainability by emphasizing complete, minimally processed meals including leafy greens, non-starchy vegetables, lean protein sources, healthy fats, and antioxidant-rich fruits.

The Keto Mediterranean Diet, which focuses on nutrient-dense foods that feed the body and mind, offers seniors a practical and pleasurable method to enhance their health and energy while eating tasty and gratifying meals.

In the next chapters of this book, we'll go deeper into the realm of the Keto Mediterranean Diet, providing you with a treasure mine of tried-and-true low-carb recipes designed to assist weight reduction, heart health, and healthy aging. With our photo guide accompanying each dish, you'll find it simple and pleasurable to cook nutritious meals that fuel your body while also satisfying your taste senses.

As we embark on our journey through the Keto Mediterranean Diet, it's important to understand the myriad benefits that arise from combining the principles of both the Ketogenic and Mediterranean approaches. By blending the best of both worlds, seniors can enjoy a wealth of health benefits that support weight loss, heart health, and overall well-being.

1. Enhanced Weight Loss

One of the most notable benefits of combining the Ketogenic and Mediterranean approaches is enhanced weight loss. The Ketogenic Diet's emphasis on low-carbohydrate, high-fat foods promotes ketosis, a metabolic state that encourages the body to burn fat for fuel. Meanwhile, the Mediterranean Diet's focus on whole, nutrient-rich foods provides a wide array of vitamins, minerals, and antioxidants that support overall health and satiety.

This mix of dietary recommendations can help you as a senior to manage their weight and promote a healthy body composition. You will successfully regulate hunger, normalize blood sugar levels, and aid fat reduction by limiting carbohydrate intake and boosting consumption of healthy fats and lean protein sources while enjoying tasty and fulfilling meals.

2. Heart Health Support

Heart health is extremely important, especially as we age. Fortunately, the Keto Mediterranean Diet has significant benefits for cardiovascular health. The Mediterranean Diet emphasizes heart-healthy fats such as olive oil, fatty fish, nuts, and seeds, which can reduce inflammation, lower cholesterol levels, and enhance blood vessel function, all of which lead to a healthier heart.

The Ketogenic Diet's ability to stabilize blood sugar levels and reduce insulin resistance may further support heart health by reducing the risk of metabolic syndrome, a cluster of conditions that increase the risk of heart disease. By combining elements of both diets, you will enjoy a heart-healthy eating pattern that promotes cardiovascular wellness and longevity.

3. Cognitive Function Support

Maintaining cognitive function is critical to overall well-being, especially as we age. The Keto Mediterranean Diet has several brain health benefits that can help seniors maintain their sharpness and focus as they age. The Mediterranean Diet, which emphasizes antioxidant-rich fruits and vegetables, omega-3 fatty acids from fish, and healthy fats from olive oil and nuts, contains essential nutrients that support brain function and protect against cognitive decline.

Furthermore, the Ketogenic Diet's capacity to increase ketone synthesis in the brain may result in additional cognitive advantages such as increased attention, mental clarity, and memory recall. Seniors who include aspects of both diets can fuel their brains with a varied range of nutrients and chemicals that support cognitive health and vibrancy.

4. Inflammation Reduction

The Ketogenic Diet's ability to reduce blood sugar levels and insulin resistance may further decrease inflammation by minimizing spikes in inflammatory markers such as C-reactive protein (CRP) and interleukin-6 (IL-6). By adopting a Keto Mediterranean eating pattern, seniors can enjoy a delicious and nutritious diet that supports overall health and reduces the risk of chronic inflammation-related conditions.

5. Longevity and Quality of Life

Chronic inflammation is a common underlying factor in many age-related diseases, including heart disease, diabetes, arthritis, and Alzheimer's disease. The Keto Mediterranean Diet offers potent anti-inflammatory properties that can help seniors reduce inflammation and protect against chronic disease. The Mediterranean Diet's emphasis on whole, unprocessed foods rich in antioxidants, vitamins, and minerals helps combat oxidative stress and inflammation throughout the body.

The Keto Mediterranean Diet aims to extend longevity and improve the quality of life for you. And by integrating the concepts of both diets, seniors may eat a broad and tasty variety of foods that feed the body, mind, and spirit. The Keto Mediterranean Diet is a sustainable and fun way to eat that promotes good aging, allowing seniors to live long into their golden years.

In the upcoming chapters of this book, we'll look at a selection of tried-and-true low-carb dishes tailored exclusively for seniors following the Keto Mediterranean Diet. With our photo guide to accompany each dish, you'll find it simple and pleasurable to cook tasty meals that promote weight reduction, heart health, and general well-being. Prepare to go on a gastronomic experience that will improve your health and energy!

The Ketogenic Diet's capacity to boost ketone synthesis in the brain may result in additional cognitive advantages like enhanced attention, mental clarity, and memory recall. Seniors who combine aspects of both diets can fuel their brains with a varied assortment of nutrients and chemicals that improve cognitive health and vibrancy.

Congratulations on taking the first step toward a healthier and more vibrant life with "Keto Mediterranean Diet Cookbook for Seniors"! This book is not just a collection of recipes; it's your comprehensive guide to embracing the Keto Mediterranean Diet and unlocking the secrets to healthy aging. Let's delve into how this book can empower you to thrive in your golden years and enjoy a life filled with vitality, wellness, and delicious food.

1. Practical Guidance for Healthy Eating

Navigating the world of nutrition can be overwhelming, especially with so many conflicting dietary recommendations. That's why this book provides you with practical guidance for healthy eating that's tailored specifically for seniors. Whether you're new to the Keto Mediterranean Diet or a seasoned pro, you'll find valuable information and tips to help you make informed choices about your diet and lifestyle.

2. Tested and Trusted Recipes for Every Meal

Gone are the days of bland and boring meals. With "Keto Mediterranean Diet Cookbook for Seniors," you'll discover a treasure trove of tested and trusted recipes for every meal of the day. From hearty breakfasts to satisfying dinners, delicious snacks to indulgent desserts, each recipe is carefully crafted to support weight loss, heart health, and overall well-being.

3. Support for Weight Loss and Heart Health

Struggling with weight management or heart health issues? You're not alone. The Keto Mediterranean Diet has been scientifically proven to support weight loss and heart health, making it an ideal dietary approach for seniors looking to improve their overall well-being. With our collection of low-carb recipes and heart-healthy ingredients, you'll have everything you need to achieve your health goals and feel your best.

4. Embrace Healthy Aging with Flavorful Food

Who says healthy eating must be bland and boring? The Keto Mediterranean Diet allows you to eat a broad selection of delectable meals that both fuel your body and satisfy your taste buds. From savory seafood to crisp salads, rich soups to indulgent desserts, each dish is intended to highlight the bright tastes of the Mediterranean while also encouraging health and life.

6. Empowerment to Take Control of Your Health

Your health is in your hands, and "Keto Mediterranean Diet Cookbook for Seniors" is here to empower you to take control of your well-being. By adopting a Keto Mediterranean eating pattern, you'll learn how to make informed choices about the foods you eat and the lifestyle habits you embrace. With our practical guidance and delicious recipes, you'll have the tools you need to thrive in your golden years and enjoy a life filled with vitality and wellness.

Chapter two

Understanding Senior Nutrition Needs

Our bodies change in a variety of ways as we age, which can have an impact on our health and well-being. From chronic diseases to age-related ailments, seniors frequently encounter a unique combination of health issues that need constant attention and control. In this chapter, we'll look at some of the most frequent health concerns among seniors and examine how the Keto Mediterranean Diet might help address and manage them

1. Weight Management

Maintaining a healthy weight becomes more difficult as we age, due to variables such as slower metabolism, hormonal changes, and decreased physical activity. Excess weight can lead to a variety of health issues, such as heart disease, diabetes, and joint discomfort. However, the Keto Mediterranean Diet is a practical answer for seniors who want to manage their weight successfully. The Keto Mediterranean Diet, which emphasizes low-carbohydrate, high-fat meals that increase satiety and stable blood sugar levels, can help seniors lose weight and maintain a healthy body weight.

2. Heart Health

Heart disease is the leading cause of death among seniors, making heart health a top priority for older adults. Factors such as high blood pressure, high cholesterol, and obesity can increase the risk of heart disease and stroke. Fortunately, the Keto Mediterranean Diet is well-suited to support heart health in seniors. Prioritizing heart-healthy fats such as olive oil, fatty fish, nuts, and seeds, and incorporating antioxidant-rich fruits and vegetables, the Keto Mediterranean Diet can help reduce inflammation, lower cholesterol levels, and improve overall cardiovascular function.

3. Type 2 Diabetes

Type 2 diabetes is a common health concern among seniors, characterized by high blood sugar levels and insulin resistance. Uncontrolled diabetes can lead to serious complications, including heart disease, nerve damage, and kidney failure. The Keto Mediterranean Diet offers a promising approach to managing type 2 diabetes in seniors. By restricting carbohydrate intake and focusing on foods that promote stable blood sugar levels, such as non-starchy vegetables, lean protein sources, and healthy fats, the Keto Mediterranean Diet can help seniors better control their blood sugar and reduce their risk of diabetes-related complications.

4. Cognitive Decline

As we become older, cognitive decline becomes more widespread, with illnesses like Alzheimer's disease and dementia impacting millions of seniors worldwide. While there is no treatment for these diseases, there is emerging evidence that nutrition and lifestyle choices play an important role in cognitive health. The Keto Mediterranean Diet is a nutrient-dense strategy to improving brain function and preventing cognitive decline in seniors. The Keto Mediterranean Diet, which includes omega-3 fatty acids from fatty fish, antioxidants from fruits and vegetables, and healthy fats from olive oil and almonds, can help seniors retain cognitive function and preserve brain.

5. Joint Health

Joint pain and arthritis are common complaints among seniors, affecting mobility and quality of life. While there is no one-size-fits-all solution for managing joint health, adopting a diet rich in anti-inflammatory foods can help alleviate symptoms and improve overall joint function. The Keto Mediterranean Diet, with its emphasis on whole, minimally processed foods and anti-inflammatory fats, offers an ideal dietary approach for seniors looking to support joint health and reduce inflammation.

6. Digestive Health

Constipation, bloating, and indigestion become increasingly common as people age, due to changes in digestion and gastrointestinal function. While medicine and lifestyle changes can help alleviate these symptoms, nutrition is essential for maintaining digestive health. The Keto Mediterranean Diet, which emphasizes fiber-rich fruits and vegetables, healthy fats, and probiotic-rich foods like yogurt and fermented veggies, can help seniors maintain regularity, enhance gut health, and ease digestive pain..

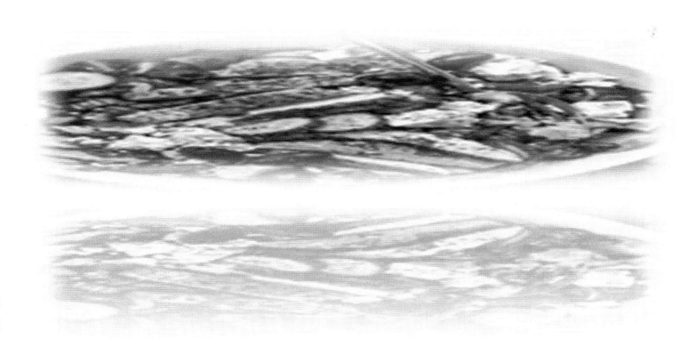

As we progress through life and into our senior years, it becomes increasingly crucial to address our dietary requirements in order to retain health, energy, and general well-being. Proper nutrition is essential for promoting healthy aging, preventing chronic illness, maintaining cognitive function, and preserving independence. In this chapter, we'll look at the fundamental nutritional requirements for seniors and how the Keto Mediterranean Diet may assist meet them, allowing you to live a robust and meaningful life far into your golden years.

1. Protein

Protein is an essential nutrient for seniors, providing the building blocks for muscle repair, immune function, and overall health. As we age, our bodies may become less efficient at utilizing protein, making it important to consume an adequate amount to maintain muscle mass and strength. The Keto Mediterranean Diet offers plenty of protein-rich options, including lean meats, poultry, fish, eggs, and legumes, ensuring seniors have the nutrients they need to stay strong and healthy.

2. Healthy Fats

Healthy fats are another important component of a senior's diet, providing essential fatty acids that support brain function, heart health, and overall well-being. The Keto Mediterranean Diet emphasizes heart-healthy fats such as olive oil, avocado, nuts, and seeds, which are rich in monounsaturated and polyunsaturated fats. These fats help reduce inflammation, lower cholesterol levels, and support cognitive function, making them an essential part of a senior's nutritional plan.

3. Fiber

Fiber is crucial for digestive health, weight management, and blood sugar control, yet many seniors struggle to consume an adequate amount in their diets. The Keto Mediterranean Diet offers plenty of fiber-rich foods such as fruits, vegetables, whole grains, and legumes, which help promote regularity, support gut health, and reduce the risk of chronic disease. By incorporating these fiber-rich foods into their meals, seniors can ensure optimal digestive function and overall well-being.

4. Vitamins and Minerals

Vitamins and minerals are essential for supporting a variety of biological activities, including immunity, bone health, and energy generation. As we age, our bodies may require more vitamins and minerals to sustain good health. The Keto Mediterranean Diet includes a variety of nutrient-dense foods such fruits, vegetables, nuts, seeds, and fish, all of which are high in vitamins and minerals necessary for good aging. Seniors may ensure they obtain the vitamins and minerals they need to flourish in their golden years by eating a variety of bright meals.

5. Hydration

Hydration is key to maintaining overall health and well-being, yet dehydration is common among seniors due to factors such as decreased thirst sensation, medication side effects, and mobility limitations. The Keto Mediterranean Diet emphasizes hydrating foods such as fruits, vegetables, and soups, which can help seniors meet their fluid needs and prevent dehydration. Additionally, seniors should aim to drink plenty of water throughout the day to stay properly hydrated and support optimal bodily function.

6. Antioxidants

Antioxidants are compounds found in foods that help protect the body against oxidative stress and inflammation, which are implicated in age-related diseases such as heart disease, cancer, and cognitive decline. The Keto Mediterranean Diet is rich in antioxidant-rich foods such as berries, leafy greens, nuts, seeds, and olive oil, which help neutralize free radicals and promote cellular health. By incorporating these antioxidant-rich foods into their diets, seniors can support their overall health and reduce the risk of chronic disease.

While we age, our health demands change, necessitating a dietary strategy that not only meets our nutritional needs but also tackles age-related issues including weight control, heart health, and cognitive function. The Keto Mediterranean Diet is a comprehensive solution designed exclusively for seniors, integrating the finest aspects of both the Ketogenic and Mediterranean diets to provide a holistic approach to good aging. In this chapter, we'll look at how the Keto Mediterranean Diet addresses seniors' special health demands and helps them thrive in their golden years.

1. Weight Management

Weight management becomes increasingly challenging as we age, yet maintaining a healthy weight is essential for overall health and well-being. The Keto Mediterranean Diet offers a practical solution for seniors looking to manage their weight effectively. By emphasizing low-carbohydrate, high-fat foods that promote satiety and stabilize blood sugar levels, the Keto Mediterranean Diet can support weight loss and help seniors achieve and maintain a healthy body weight. Additionally, the Mediterranean Diet's emphasis on whole, nutrient-rich foods ensures seniors receive the essential vitamins, minerals, and antioxidants they need to support their overall health and well-being.

2. Heart Health

Heart disease is a leading cause of death among seniors, making heart health a top priority for older adults. The Keto Mediterranean Diet is well-suited to support heart health in seniors by emphasizing heart-healthy fats such as olive oil, fatty fish, nuts, and seeds, and incorporating antioxidant-rich fruits and vegetables. These foods help reduce inflammation, lower cholesterol levels, and improve overall cardiovascular function, reducing the risk of heart disease and stroke. Additionally, the Ketogenic Diet's ability to stabilize blood sugar levels and reduce insulin resistance may further support heart health by minimizing spikes in inflammatory markers such as C-reactive protein (CRP) and interleukin-6 (IL-6).

3. Cognitive Function

Maintaining cognitive function is critical to general well-being, especially as we age. The Keto Mediterranean Diet has various brain health advantages that can help seniors maintain their sharpness and attention as they age. The Mediterranean Diet, which emphasizes antioxidant-rich fruits and vegetables, omega-3 fatty acids from fish, and healthy fats from olive oil and almonds, contains vital nutrients that enhance brain function and protect against cognitive decline. Furthermore, the Ketogenic Diet's capacity to boost ketone synthesis in the brain may result in additional cognitive advantages such as increased attention, mental clarity, and memory recall.

4. Joint Health

Joint pain and arthritis are common complaints among seniors, affecting mobility and quality of life. The Keto Mediterranean Diet can help support joint health in seniors by reducing inflammation and providing essential nutrients for joint repair and maintenance. The Mediterranean Diet's emphasis on anti-inflammatory foods such as fruits, vegetables, and olive oil helps reduce inflammation throughout the body, alleviating joint pain and stiffness. Additionally, the Ketogenic Diet's ability to promote weight loss and stabilize blood sugar levels may further support joint health by reducing the load on the joints and minimizing inflammation.

5. Digestive Health

Digestive issues such as constipation, bloating, and indigestion become more prevalent with age, due to changes in digestion and gastrointestinal function. The Keto Mediterranean Diet can help support digestive health in seniors by emphasizing fiber-rich foods such as fruits, vegetables, whole grains, and legumes. These foods help promote regularity, support gut health, and reduce the risk of chronic disease. Additionally, the Mediterranean Diet's emphasis on healthy fats such as olive oil and nuts helps lubricate the digestive tract and support optimal digestion.

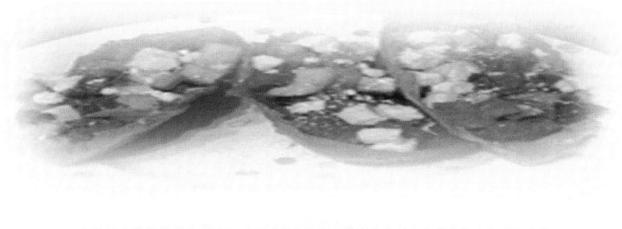

6. Overall Well Being

Ultimately, the goal of the Keto Mediterranean Diet is to promote overall health and well-being in seniors, empowering them to live their best lives in their golden years. By incorporating elements of both the Ketogenic and Mediterranean diets, the Keto Mediterranean Diet provides seniors with a balanced and sustainable approach to eating that supports their unique health needs. With delicious and nutritious recipes tailored specifically for seniors, along with a picture guide for easy cooking, the Keto Mediterranean Diet Cookbook for Seniors is your comprehensive resource for promoting weight loss, heart health, and overall vitality through delicious and nutritious food.

Chapter Three

Essential Kitchen Tools and Ingredients

Must-Have Kitchen Equipment for Seniors

Creating delicious and nutritious meals is made easier with the right kitchen equipment. Whether you're a seasoned chef or new to the culinary world, having the right tools at your disposal can make meal preparation more efficient, enjoyable, and safe. In this chapter, we'll explore the must-have kitchen equipment for seniors embarking on their Keto Mediterranean Diet journey, ensuring that you have everything you need to cook up a storm and delight your taste buds.

1. Chef's Knife

A high-quality chef's knife is an essential tool for any home cook, allowing you to chop, slice, and dice with precision and ease. Look for a chef's knife with a comfortable handle and a sharp blade that feels balanced in your hand. Investing in a good quality chef's knife will make meal preparation safer and more efficient, allowing you to tackle a wide variety of ingredients with confidence.

2. Cutting Board

A durable cutting board provides a stable surface for chopping fruits, vegetables, and other ingredients. Opt for a cutting board made from wood or plastic, which are easy to clean and maintain. Choose a size that fits comfortably on your countertop and provides ample space for food preparation. Having a dedicated cutting board will help protect your countertops and make clean-up a breeze.

3. Nonstick Skillet

A nonstick skillet is a versatile piece of cookware that's perfect for sautéing, frying, and cooking a wide range of dishes. Look for a nonstick skillet with a comfortable handle and a durable nonstick coating that allows for easy food release and cleanup. Choose a size that suits your cooking needs, whether you're preparing a single serving or cooking for a crowd. A nonstick skillet is a kitchen essential that will make cooking healthy meals a breeze.

4. Oven Safe Baking Dish

An oven-safe baking dish is perfect for preparing casseroles, roasted vegetables, and baked desserts. Look for a baking dish made from durable materials such as ceramic or glass, which can withstand high temperatures without warping or cracking. Choose a size that fits comfortably in your oven and provides ample space for your favorite recipes. Having an oven-safe baking dish on hand will allow you to create delicious and nutritious meals with ease.

5. Blender or Food Processor

A blender or food processor is a versatile tool that's perfect for creating smoothies, sauces, soups, and more. Look for a blender or food processor with multiple speed settings and sharp blades that can handle a variety of ingredients. Choose a size that suits your kitchen space and cooking needs, whether you're blending single servings or preparing large batches of food. Having a blender or food processor on hand will allow you to easily incorporate fruits, vegetables, and other nutritious ingredients into your meals.

6. Measuring Cups and Spoons

Precision measurements are essential for effective cooking and baking. Invest in a set of measuring cups and spoons to guarantee that your recipes come out perfectly every time. Look for a set with a choice of sizes, ranging from tablespoons to cups, to suit diverse ingredients and serving amounts. Having measuring cups and spoons on hand will allow you to follow recipes precisely and obtain consistent results.

7. Slow Cooker or Instant Pot

A slow cooker or Instant Pot is a convenient tool for preparing hearty soups, stews, and one-pot meals with minimal effort. Look for a slow cooker or Instant Pot with multiple cooking settings and a programmable timer for added convenience. Choose a size that suits your cooking needs and kitchen space, whether you're cooking for one or feeding a crowd. Having a slow cooker or Instant Pot on hand will allow you to enjoy delicious and nutritious meals with minimal hands-on cooking time.

8. Salad Spinner

A salad spinner is a handy tool for washing and drying leafy greens, herbs, and other delicate ingredients. Look for a salad spinner with a removable basket and easy-to-use crank or lever mechanism. Choose a size that fits comfortably in your sink and provides ample space for your ingredients. Having a salad spinner on hand will make it easy to prepare fresh salads and vegetable dishes with ease.

9. Food Storage Containers

Food storage containers are essential for storing leftovers, meal prep ingredients, and batch-cooked meals. Look for containers that are durable, leak-proof, and freezer-safe, allowing you to store food safely and efficiently. Choose a variety of sizes to accommodate different portion sizes and storage needs. Having food storage containers on hand will help you reduce food waste and make meal planning and prep a breeze.

10. Can Opener

A reliable can opener is a kitchen essential for opening canned goods such as beans, tomatoes, and soups. Look for a can opener with a comfortable grip and sharp cutting wheel that easily pierces cans without leaving sharp edges. Choose a handheld or electric can opener that suits your preferences and kitchen space. Having a can opener on hand will ensure that you have access to pantry staples whenever you need them.

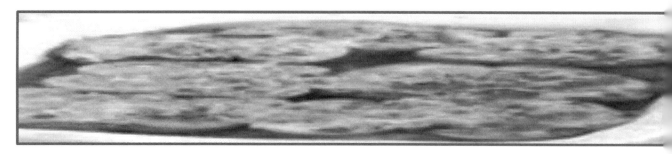

Key Ingredients for a Keto Mediterranean Pantry

Stocking your pantry with the right ingredients is essential for success on the Keto Mediterranean Diet. By having a well-stocked pantry, you'll be able to whip up delicious and nutritious meals with ease, all while supporting your weight loss and heart health goals. In this chapter, we'll explore the key ingredients for a Keto Mediterranean pantry, ensuring that you have everything you need to create flavorful and satisfying dishes that nourish your body and soul.

1. Olive Oil

Olive oil is a staple ingredient in the Mediterranean diet, prized for its heart-healthy fats and rich flavor. Opt for extra-virgin olive oil, which is minimally processed and retains the highest levels of antioxidants and nutrients. Use olive oil for cooking, dressing salads, and drizzling over roasted vegetables for a flavorful and nutritious addition to your meals.

2. Nuts and Seeds

Nuts and seeds are nutrient-rich powerhouses that provide essential fats, protein, and fiber. Stock your pantry with a variety of nuts and seeds such as almonds, walnuts, pistachios, pumpkin seeds, and chia seeds. Enjoy them as a snack, sprinkle them over salads, or incorporate them into your favorite recipes for added crunch and flavor.

3. Canned Fish

Canned fish such as tuna, salmon, and sardines are convenient and versatile pantry staples that are packed with heart-healthy omega-3 fatty acids. Look for canned fish that's packed in water or olive oil and opt for varieties that are sustainably sourced. Use canned fish to make salads, sandwiches, or pasta dishes for a quick and nutritious meal.

4. Canned Tomatoes

Canned tomatoes are a pantry essential that adds depth and richness to a wide variety of dishes. Stock your pantry with canned diced tomatoes, tomato sauce, and tomato paste to use in soups, stews, sauces, and casseroles. Look for canned tomatoes that are low in added sugars and sodium for a healthier option.

5. Legumes

Legumes such as chickpeas, lentils, and beans are nutrient-dense foods that provide protein, fiber, and essential vitamins and minerals. Stock your pantry with dried or canned legumes to use in soups, salads, and main dishes. Opt for low-carb options such as chickpea pasta or black soybeans for a Keto-friendly twist on classic recipes.

6. Herbs and Spices

Herbs and spices are the secret to adding flavor and depth to your dishes without the need for excess salt or added sugars. Stock your pantry with a variety of herbs and spices such as basil, oregano, thyme, rosemary, cumin, paprika, and turmeric. Experiment with different flavor combinations to create delicious and aromatic meals that tantalize your taste buds.

7. Low Carb Grains and Pasta

While traditional grains and pasta are high in carbohydrates, there are plenty of low-carb alternatives that are perfect for the Keto Mediterranean Diet. Stock your pantry with options such as almond flour, coconut flour, cauliflower rice, and spiralized vegetables such as zucchini or squash. These low-carb alternatives can be used to create nutritious and satisfying dishes that are perfect for seniors following the Keto Mediterranean Diet.

8. Vinegar

Vinegar adds acidity and brightness to dishes, enhancing their flavor and complexity. Stock your pantry with a variety of vinegars such as balsamic vinegar, red wine vinegar, apple cider vinegar, and white wine vinegar. Use vinegar to make salad dressings, marinades, and sauces, or drizzle it over roasted vegetables for a burst of flavor.

9. Dark Chocolate

Dark chocolate is a delicious and satisfying treat that can be enjoyed in moderation on the Keto Mediterranean Diet. Look for dark chocolate with a high cocoa content (70% or higher) and minimal added sugars. Enjoy a square of dark chocolate as an occasional indulgence or use it to add richness and depth to your favorite desserts.

10. Coconut Milk

Coconut milk is a creamy and versatile ingredient that adds richness and flavor to both sweet and savory dishes. Stock your pantry with canned coconut milk to use in curries, soups, smoothies, and desserts. Opt for unsweetened coconut milk to keep added sugars to a minimum and choose full-fat varieties for a richer texture and flavor.

Shopping Tips and Ingredient Substitutions for Seniors on a Budget

Eating healthily on a budget is possible with the right strategies and mindset. As seniors, it's important to make smart choices when it comes to grocery shopping and meal planning, ensuring that you can enjoy nutritious and delicious meals without breaking the bank. In this chapter, we'll explore practical shopping tips and ingredient substitutions for seniors on a budget, helping you make the most of your grocery budget while still enjoying the benefits of the Keto Mediterranean Diet.

1. Plan Your Meals

Before you go to the grocery store, spend some time planning your weekly meals. Look for dishes that employ comparable goods to save waste and stretch your buying budget. Consider including low-cost mainstays like beans, lentils, and canned veggies into your meals to help you stretch your food budget.

2. Shop the Sales

Take advantage of deals and discounts to save money on your food purchases. Keep a look out for weekly promotions, buy-one, get-one-free deals, and seasonal food savings. Consider buying pantry basics like canned foods, cereals, and pasta on sale to save money in the long term.

3. Buy in Bulk

Purchasing in bulk can help you save money on pantry basics and nonperishable products. Look for bulk bins at your local grocery store or join a wholesale club to get better deals on grains, nuts, seeds, and dried fruits. To prevent wasting food, buy only what you can consume before it spoils.

4. Choose Frozen and Canned Produce

Frozen and canned produce are often more budget-friendly than fresh produce and can be just as nutritious. Look for frozen fruits and vegetables without added sugars or sauces, and opt for canned vegetables with no added salt. These options are convenient, versatile, and perfect for incorporating into your favorite Keto Mediterranean recipes.

5. Substitute Affordable Proteins

Protein can be one of the most expensive items on your grocery list, but there are plenty of budget-friendly options to choose from. Consider substituting affordable proteins such as eggs, canned tuna or salmon, tofu, tempeh, and legumes for more expensive cuts of meat. These options are just as nutritious and versatile, allowing you to enjoy a variety of protein-rich meals without breaking the bank.

6. Use Seasonal Produce

Seasonal vegetables is typically more plentiful and less costly than out-of-season kinds. Take advantage of seasonal fruits and vegetables to reduce your grocery expenditure while enjoying the freshest, most delicious foods. To find out what's in season and on sale, go to your local farmers' market or check your grocery store's weekly specials.

7. Make Your Own Convenience Foods

Pre-packaged convenience foods might be handy, but they are sometimes rather expensive. Save money by preparing your own convenience meals at home. Cook in batches and freeze individual servings for quick and simple dinners throughout the week. Make your own salad dressings, sauces, and marinades with pantry basics to save money and have more control over the ingredients.

8. Compare Prices and Brands

Compare prices and brands to ensure you get the greatest value for your money. Consider using store brands and generic alternatives to name brands to save money without losing quality. Keep an eye out for unit pricing and price-per-ounce labels to help you make more educated choices and extend your food budget.

9. Avoid Impulse Purchases

Stick to your grocery list and avoid impulse purchases to prevent overspending. Before heading to the store, make a list of the items you need and stick to it. Avoid shopping when you're hungry, as hunger can lead to impulse purchases of unhealthy and expensive items. By planning ahead and sticking to your list, you can avoid unnecessary spending and stay on budget.

10. Grow Your Own

Consider growing your own fruits, vegetables, and herbs to save money on your grocery bill. Even if you don't have a large garden, you can grow herbs in pots on your windowsill or balcony. Fresh herbs add flavor and depth to your meals and can be grown inexpensively at home. Plus, gardening is a rewarding and therapeutic hobby that provides exercise and fresh air.

Ingredient Substitutions for you on a Budget:

- ✓ Instead of fresh herbs, use dried herbs and spices.
- ✓ Substitute canned beans for dried beans to save time and money.
- ✓ Use frozen vegetables in place of fresh when fresh produce is out of season or expensive.
- ✓ Substitute cheaper cuts of meat for more expensive cuts in recipes.
- ✓ Use cheaper protein sources such as eggs, tofu, and canned fish in place of expensive meats.
- ✓ Make your own broth using vegetable scraps and leftover bones to save money on store-bought broth.
- ✓ Use water or broth instead of wine in recipes to save money and reduce alcohol consumption.
- ✓ Substitute almond flour or coconut flour for wheat flour in baking recipes to make them gluten-free and budget-friendly.

With these practical shopping tips and ingredient substitutions, seniors can enjoy delicious and nutritious meals while staying within their budget. By planning ahead, making smart choices, and being mindful of where you spend your grocery dollars, you can eat well without breaking the bank on the Keto Mediterranean Diet.

Chapter Four

Meal Planning Strategies for Seniors

Simple Meal Planning Techniques for Seniors

Meal planning is a powerful tool that can help seniors eat healthily, save time, and reduce stress in the kitchen. By taking the time to plan your meals ahead of time, you can ensure that you have nutritious and delicious options on hand, making it easier to stick to your Keto Mediterranean Diet goals. In this chapter, we'll explore simple meal planning techniques for seniors, helping you streamline your meal preparation process and enjoy healthy, satisfying meals every day.

1. Set Realistic Goals

Before you start meal planning, take some time to set realistic goals for yourself. Consider factors such as your dietary preferences, nutritional needs, cooking skills, and budget. Determine how many meals you'll need to plan for each week and whether you'll be cooking for yourself or others. Setting realistic goals will help you create a meal plan that's tailored to your individual needs and preferences.

2. Choose Your Recipes

Once you've set your goals, it's time to choose your recipes for the week. Look for recipes that align with your Keto Mediterranean Diet goals and incorporate a variety of flavors, textures, and nutrients. Consider factors such as seasonality, ingredient availability, and cooking time when selecting your recipes. Choose a mix of familiar favorites and new dishes to keep things interesting and exciting.

3. Make a Shopping List

Once you've chosen your recipes, it's time to make a shopping list. Take inventory of the ingredients you already have on hand and make a list of the items you'll need to purchase. Organize your list by category (e.g., produce, proteins, pantry staples) to make shopping more efficient. Be sure to include any special ingredients or kitchen equipment you'll need for your recipes.

4. Prep Ahead

To save time and streamline your meal preparation process, consider prepping some ingredients ahead of time. Wash and chop vegetables, marinate meats, and prepare sauces and dressings in advance so they're ready to go when you need them. Store prepped ingredients in airtight containers in the refrigerator or freezer to keep them fresh until you're ready to use them.

5. Batch Cook

Batch cooking is an excellent method to save time while ensuring that you always have nutritious meals on hand. Select one day every week to batch cook a couple meals in big amounts, then separate them into individual portions and store in the refrigerator or freezer. Batch cooking allows you to enjoy delicious meals without having to cook them from scratch each day.

6. Embrace Simplicity

When it comes to meal planning, simplicity is essential. Concentrate on dishes that are simple to create, use few ingredients, and can be produced in huge quantities. Choose recipes that employ adaptable ingredients that can be tailored to your specific tastes and nutritional needs. Do not be hesitant to simplify recipes or substitute ingredients based on what you have on hand.

7. Use Leftovers Wisely

Leftovers are a wonderful resource for meal planning. Instead of wasting leftovers, use them in future meals. Use leftover roasted veggies in salads or omelettes, leftover chicken in sandwiches or wraps, and leftover grains in grain bowls or stir-fries. To make the best use of your leftovers, be creative and think outside the box.

8. Plan for Variety

Variety is the spice of life, so be sure to plan for a variety of flavors, textures, and cuisines in your meal plan. Incorporate a mix of different proteins, vegetables, grains, and spices to keep things interesting and exciting. Experiment with new ingredients and recipes to expand your culinary horizons and discover new favorites.

9. Be Flexible

While meal preparation might help you stick to your Keto Mediterranean Diet objectives, it's also crucial to be adaptable. Life may be unpredictable, and plans often alter. Be prepared to modify your meal plan as required due to scheduling changes, unforeseen events, and ingredient availability. Don't worry about following to your plan precisely; instead, focus on making good choices and enjoying the process.

10. Enjoy the Process

Above all, remember to enjoy the process of meal planning and cooking. Mealtime should be a time to nourish your body and soul, so savor the experience of preparing and enjoying delicious, homemade meals. Get creative in the kitchen, experiment with new flavors and ingredients, and take pride in knowing that you're taking control of your health and well-being through mindful meal planning.

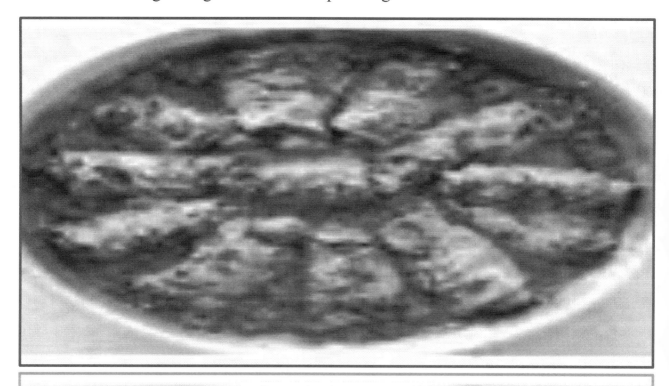

Weekly Meal Prep Tips to Save Time and Energy

Meal prep is a game-changer when it comes to saving time, reducing stress, and staying on track with your Keto Mediterranean Diet goals. By dedicating a little time each week to preparing meals and ingredients in advance, you can enjoy delicious and nutritious meals throughout the week with minimal effort. In this section, we'll explore weekly meal prep tips to help seniors save time and energy in the kitchen, making healthy eating easier and more enjoyable than ever before.

1. Set Aside Time Each Week

Start by setting aside a specific day and time each week for meal prep. Choose a day when you have some free time and won't be rushed, such as Sunday afternoon or a quiet weekday evening. Block off a few hours on your calendar dedicated to meal prep, and treat it as an important appointment that you can't miss.

2. Plan Your Meals

Before you start meal prepping, take some time to plan out your meals for the week. Choose recipes that are suitable for batch cooking and can be easily portioned out into individual servings. Consider factors such as seasonality, ingredient availability, and dietary preferences when selecting your recipes. Make a list of the ingredients you'll need for each recipe and create a shopping list to ensure you have everything you need on hand.

3. Stock Up on Storage Containers

Invest in a variety of storage containers in different shapes and sizes to store your prepped ingredients and meals. Choose containers that are microwave-safe, dishwasher-safe, and freezer-safe for maximum versatility. Look for containers with tight-fitting lids to keep your food fresh and prevent leaks and spills. Having a selection of storage containers on hand will make portioning out meals and storing leftovers a breeze.

4. Prep Ingredients in Advance

Take advantage of your meal prep time to wash, chop, and portion out ingredients in advance. Wash and chop vegetables, marinate meats, and portion out grains and legumes so they're ready to go when you need them. Store prepped ingredients in individual containers or zip-top bags in the refrigerator or freezer to keep them fresh until you're ready to use them.

5. Batch Cook Meals

Batch cooking is a time-saving technique that involves cooking large quantities of food at once and portioning it out into individual servings. Choose one or two recipes to batch cook each week, such as soups, stews, casseroles, or grain bowls. Cook the recipes in large batches and portion them out into individual containers for easy grab-and-go meals throughout the week.

6. Mix and Match Components

Keep things interesting by mixing and matching components to create a variety of meals throughout the week. Cook a big batch of protein, such as grilled chicken or roasted salmon, and pair it with different vegetables, grains, and sauces to create a variety of meals. Get creative and experiment with different flavor combinations to keep your meals exciting and satisfying.

7. Use Time Saving Kitchen Tools

Invest in time-saving kitchen tools and appliances to streamline your meal prep process. Consider tools such as a slow cooker, Instant Pot, food processor, or immersion blender to make cooking and meal prep easier and more efficient. Look for tools that can perform multiple functions to save space and money in your kitchen.

8. Prep Snacks and Breakfasts

Don't forget to prep snacks and breakfasts in advance to save time during busy mornings and snack times. Wash and chop fruits and vegetables, portion out nuts and seeds, and prepare grab-and-go snacks such as energy balls or homemade granola bars. Pre-portion smoothie ingredients into individual bags and store them in the freezer for quick and easy breakfasts on the go.

9. Label and Organize

Stay organized by labeling your storage containers with the contents and date of preparation. Use labels or masking tape and a permanent marker to clearly mark each container, making it easy to identify what's inside and when it was prepared. Store similar items together in your refrigerator or freezer to make mealtime prep and cleanup a breeze.

10. Embrace Imperfection

Remember that meal prep doesn't have to be perfect. It's okay if you don't have every meal planned out or if things don't go exactly as planned. The goal of meal prep is to save time and energy and make healthy eating easier, so don't stress about getting everything perfect. Focus on doing what works for you and your schedule, and adjust as needed along the way.

How to Tailor Meal Plans to Your Individual Needs and Preferences

One size does not fit all when it comes to meal planning. As seniors, it's important to tailor your meal plans to your individual needs and preferences to ensure that you're eating healthily and enjoying your meals. By taking into account factors such as dietary restrictions, taste preferences, and nutritional requirements, you can create meal plans that are personalized to your unique needs and goals. In this chapter, we'll explore how to tailor meal plans to your individual needs and preferences, helping you create delicious and satisfying meals that support your health and well-being on the Keto Mediterranean Diet.

1. Consider Your Dietary Needs

The first step in tailoring your meal plan is to consider your dietary needs and any restrictions you may have. Take into account factors such as food allergies, intolerances, medical conditions, and personal preferences when planning your meals. If you have specific dietary restrictions, such as gluten intolerance or lactose intolerance, be sure to choose recipes and ingredients that accommodate those needs.

2. Assess Your Nutritional Requirements

Next, assess your nutritional requirements and make sure your meal plan provides the nutrients your body needs to thrive. Consider factors such as your age, gender, activity level, and any health conditions you may have when planning your meals. Aim to include a balance of macronutrients (carbohydrates, proteins, and fats) and micronutrients (vitamins and minerals) in your meals to support overall health and well-being.

3. Choose Foods You Enjoy

One of the keys to sticking to a meal plan is to choose foods that you enjoy eating. Take some time to think about your favorite foods, flavors, and cuisines, and incorporate them into your meal plan whenever possible. Experiment with different recipes and ingredients to keep things interesting and exciting, and don't be afraid to get creative in the kitchen.

4. Listen to Your Body

Pay attention to how different foods make you feel and adjust your meal plan accordingly. If certain foods or ingredients make you feel bloated, sluggish, or uncomfortable, consider eliminating them from your meal plan or reducing your intake. Conversely, if you find that certain foods make you feel energized and satisfied, include them more frequently in your meals.

5. Plan for Flexibility

Life can be unpredictable, so it's important to plan for flexibility in your meal plan. Allow for some wiggle room in your plan to accommodate changes in schedule, unexpected events, and last-minute cravings. Be open to making adjustments to your meal plan as needed and don't stress about sticking to it perfectly. The goal is to create a plan that works for you and your lifestyle, so be flexible and adaptable.

6. Incorporate Variety

Variety is key to a healthy and satisfying meal plan. Incorporate a variety of different foods, flavors, and textures into your meals to keep things interesting and ensure you're getting a wide range of nutrients. Experiment with different fruits, vegetables, proteins, grains, and spices to create flavorful and nutritious meals that you look forward to eating.

7. Plan for Occasional Treats

While it's important to prioritize healthy, nutrient-dense foods in your meal plan, it's also okay to indulge in occasional treats and splurges. Allow yourself to enjoy your favorite foods in moderation and don't deprive yourself of the foods you love. Incorporate treats into your meal plan occasionally and savor them mindfully, enjoying every bite without guilt or restriction.

8. Be Realistic

Finally, be realistic about your meal planning goals and expectations. Don't strive for perfection or put too much pressure on yourself to stick to your plan perfectly. Life happens, and it's okay if things don't always go according to plan. Focus on making healthy choices most of the time and be kind to yourself when things don't go as planned.

We will soon move to the kitchen in the next page, but before then I know you have started admiring to appreciate the dishes and thoughts in this book. I'd like to recommend two more publications that will help you on developing your health done by us.

1. Discover the "DASH Diet Mediterranean Weight Loss Solution".

Consider supplementing your existing diet with the DASH Diet Mediterranean Weight Loss Solution. This book mixes DASH principles with Mediterranean tastes, providing:

Balanced, Nutrient-Rich Recipes: Ideal for cardiovascular health and long-term weight reduction.

Practical tips: Simple ways for reducing salt and increasing nutrient-dense meals.

2. Adopt the "Sugar Elimination Diet for Beginners"

Consider continuing with the Sugar Elimination Diet for Beginners. Reducing sugar consumption can significantly improve your health, and this book offers:

Recipes for Beginners: Simple meals to minimize sugar cravings.

Practical Advice: Tips for detecting and eliminating hidden sugars.

Why Do These Books Matter?

Both of these books are intended to improve your entire health and well-being by providing:

- ✓ Holistic health is a balanced approach to diet.
- ✓ Diverse Recipes: More tasty, health-promoting meals.
- ✓ Long-term behaviors for improved health are examples of sustainable change.

To get these books are very simple, just follow the easy steps in the next page:

Kindly bring out your phone and:

1. Locate the QR of the required book

2. Open your smartphone QR scanner

3. Wait a little, notification will appear on your screen with a link or prompt

4. Tap the notification or link that appears

5. Follow the on-screen instruction to navigate

For more book like this:

Let's look at some delicious meals to help us start the day with energy and goodness.

Chapter Four

Breakfasts to Start Your Day Right

Good morning elders!

Breakfast is considered the most essential meal of the day. Let's look at some delicious meals to help us start the day with energy and goodness. Here are seven stimulating Keto Mediterranean breakfast dishes just for you:

Days	Recipes	Prep Time (Minutes)	Colories	Servings
Day 1	Mediterranean Veggie Omelette	10	250	1
Day 2	Greek Yogurt with Berries and Almonds	5	200	1
Day 3	Avocado and Smoked Salmon Toast	5	300	1
Day 4	Mediterranean Egg Muffins	15	150	2
Day 5	Greek Yogurt Parfait with Nuts and Honey	5	250	1
Day 6	Spinach and Tomato Frittata	20	180	4
Day 7	Keto Mediterranean Breakfast Salad	15	220	1

Mediterranean Veggie Omelette

Calories: 250 calories.   **Prep Time: 10 minutes.**

Servings: 1

INGREDIENTS

1. 2 large eggs
2. 1/4 cup diced tomatoes
3. 1/4 cup chopped spinach
4. 1/4 cup sliced bell peppers
5. Salt and pepper to taste
6. 1 teaspoon olive oil

HEALTH BENEFITS

It is high in protein, vitamins, and antioxidants. Supports muscle health and overall well-being.

DIRECTIONS

1. In a bowl, whisk together the eggs and season with salt and pepper.

2. Heat the olive oil in a skillet over medium heat.

3. Add the tomatoes, spinach, and bell peppers and sauté until soft.

4. Pour eggs into the skillet and heat until set.

5. Fold the omelette and serve hot.

Greek Yogurt with Berries and Almonds

Calories: 200 calories.   **Prep Time: 5 minutes..**

Servings: 1

INGREDIENTS

1. 1/2 cup Greek yogurt
2. 1/4 cup mixed berries
3. 1 tablespoon sliced almonds
4. 1 teaspoon honey (optional)

HEALTH BENEFITS

It is Rich in probiotics, antioxidants, and healthy fats. It also Supports gut health and provides energy.

DIRECTIONS

1. In a bowl, combine Greek yogurt and mixed berries.

2. Top with sliced almonds and drizzle with honey if desired.

3. Serve chilled

Avocado and Smoked Salmon Toast

Calories: 300 calories.　　　　**Prep Time: 5 minutes.**

Servings: 1

INGREDIENTS

1. 1 slice whole-grain bread
2. 1/4 avocado, sliced
3. 2 slices smoked salmon
4. 1 teaspoon capers
5. Fresh dill for garnish

HEALTH BENEFITS

It is Rich in omega-3 fatty acids, fiber, and vitamins. Supports heart health and brain function.

DIRECTIONS

1. Toast the bread until golden brown.

2. Spread avocado on the toast.

3. Top with smoked salmon and capers.

4. Garnish with fresh dill.

5. Serve immediately.

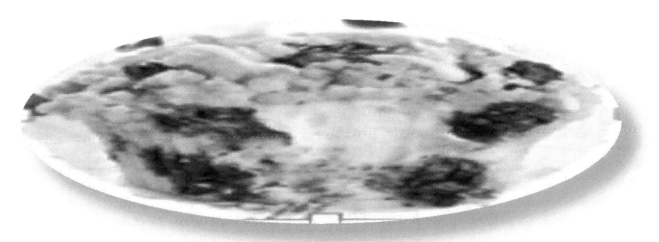

Mediterranean Egg Muffins

Calories: 150 calories.   **Prep Time: 15 minutes.**

Servings: 2

INGREDIENTS

1. 4 large eggs
2. 1/4 cup diced tomatoes
3. 1/4 cup chopped spinach
4. 1/4 cup crumbled feta cheese
5. Salt and pepper to taste

HEALTH BENEFITS

It is high in protein, vitamins, and minerals. Supports muscle health and bone density.

DIRECTIONS

1. Preheat oven to 350°F (175°C).

2. In a bowl, whisk eggs and season with salt and pepper.

3. Stir in tomatoes, spinach, and feta cheese.

4. Pour mixture into muffin tin.

5. Bake for 15-20 minutes or until set.

6. Serve warm.

Greek Yogurt Parfait with Nuts and Honey

Calories: 250 calories.   **Prep Time: 5 minutes.**

Servings: 1

INGREDIENTS

1. 1/2 cup Greek yogurt
2. 1/4 cup granola
3. 1 tablespoon chopped nuts
4. 1 teaspoon honey

1. In a glass, layer Greek yogurt, granola, and chopped nuts.
2. Drizzle with honey.
3. Repeat layers.
4. Serve chilled.

HEALTH BENEFITS

It is rich in probiotics, fiber, and antioxidants. Supports digestion and provides sustained energy.

Spinach and Tomato Frittata

Calories: 180 calories.

Prep Time: 20 minutes.

Servings: 4

INGREDIENTS

1. 6 large eggs
2. 1/4 cup milk or almond milk
3. 1 cup chopped spinach
4. 1/2 cup diced tomatoes
5. 1/4 cup shredded mozzarella
6. cheese Salt and pepper to taste

HEALTH BENEFITS

It is high in protein, vitamins, and antioxidants. Supports muscle health and overall well-being.

DIRECTIONS

1. Whisk eggs in a bowl and season with salt and pepper.

2. Heat olive oil in a skillet over medium heat.

3. Add tomatoes, spinach, and bell peppers, sauté until tender.

4. Pour eggs into the skillet and heat until set.

5. Fold the omelette and serve hot.

Keto Mediterranean Breakfast Salad

Calories: 220 calories.   **Prep Time: 15 minutes.**

Servings: 1

INGREDIENTS

1. 2 cups mixed greens
2. 1 hard-boiled egg, sliced
3. 1/4 cup cucumber, diced
4. 1/4 cup cherry tomatoes, halved
5. 2 tablespoons olives
6. 1 tablespoon feta cheese
7. 1 tablespoon olive oil
8. 1 tablespoon balsamic vinegar
9. Salt and pepper to taste

DIRECTIONS

1 .In a bowl, combine mixed greens, cucumber, tomatoes, olives, and feta cheese.

2. Drizzle with olive oil and balsamic vinegar.

3. Season with salt and pepper.

4. Toss gently to coat.

5. Top with sliced hard-boiled egg.

6. Serve chilled.

Nourishing Lunch Recipes for you!

Hello there! Let's make lunchtime easy and tasty. We'll discuss several delicious lunch options that will keep us filled and energized all afternoon. Here are seven nutritious Keto Mediterranean lunch dishes designed for seniors:

Days	Recipes	Prep Time (Minutes)	Colories	Servings
Day 1	Greek Chicken Salad	30	380	2
Day 2	Mediterranean Stuffed Bell Peppers	20	250	2
Day 3	Greek Turkey Lettuce Wraps	15	280	2
Day 4	Mediterranean Tuna Salad	10	220	2
Day 5	Greek Zucchini Boats	25	280	2
Day 6	Mediterranean Tuna Salad	10	220	2
Day 7	Mediterranean Eggplant and Chickpea Salad	30	250	2

Greek Chicken Salad

Calories: 380 calories.   **Prep Time: 30 minutes.**

Servings: 2

INGREDIENTS

1. 2 cups mixed greens
2. 1 cooked chicken breast, shredded
3. 1/4 cup cherry tomatoes, halved
4. 1/4 cup cucumber, sliced
5. 1/4 cup Kalamata olives
6. 2 tablespoons crumbled feta cheese
7. 2 tablespoons extra-virgin olive oil
8. 1 tablespoon red wine vinegar
9. Salt and pepper to taste

DIRECTIONS

1. In a large bowl, combine mixed greens, shredded chicken, cherry tomatoes, cucumber, olives, and feta cheese.

2. In a small mixing bowl, combine olive oil, red wine vinegar, salt, and pepper to prepare the dressing.

3. Drizzle salad with the dressing and gently toss to coat.

4. Serve immediately.

Mediterranean Stuffed Bell Peppers

Calories: 250 calories.   **Prep Time: 20 minutes.**

Servings: 2

INGREDIENTS

1. 2 large bell peppers
2. 1/2 cup cooked quinoa
3. 1/4 cup diced tomatoes
4. 1/4 cup chopped spinach
5. 1/4 cup crumbled feta cheese
6. 2 tablespoons chopped fresh parsley
7. 1 tablespoon olive oil
8. Salt and pepper to taste 1 tablespoon olive oil
9. Salt and pepper to taste

DIRECTIONS

1. Preheat the oven to 375°F (190°C).

2. Cut off the bell pepper tops and remove the seeds and membranes.

3. In a bowl, mix together cooked quinoa, diced tomatoes, chopped spinach, crumbled feta cheese, chopped parsley, olive oil, salt, and pepper.

4. Stuff the mixture into the bell peppers.

5. Place the stuffed peppers in a baking dish and bake for 25-30 minutes, or until the peppers are tender.

6. Serve hot..

Greek Turkey Lettuce Wraps

Calories: 280 calories.   **Prep Time: 15 minutes.**

Servings: 2

INGREDIENTS

1. 1/2 lb ground turkey
2. 1/4 cup diced tomatoes
3. 1/4 cup diced cucumber
4. 1/4 cup diced red onion
5. 2 tablespoons chopped Kalamata olives
6. 2 tablespoons crumbled feta cheese
7. 1 tablespoon extra-virgin olive oil
8. 1 tablespoon lemon juice
9. Salt and pepper to taste
10. Butter lettuce leaves for wrapping

DIRECTIONS

1. In a skillet, cook ground turkey over medium heat until browned and cooked through.

2. In a bowl, mix together diced tomatoes, cucumber, red onion, olives, feta cheese, olive oil, lemon juice, salt, and pepper.

3. Spoon the turkey mixture onto butter lettuce leaves.

4. Roll up the leaves to form wraps.

Mediterranean Tuna Salad

Calories: 220 calories   **Prep Time: 10 minutes**

Servings: 2

INGREDIENTS

1. 2 cans (5 oz each) drained tuna,
2. 1/4 cup diced cucumber
3. 1/4 cup diced red onion
4. 1/4 cup diced bell peppers
5. 2 tablespoons chopped Kalamata olives
6. 2 tablespoons chopped fresh parsley
7. 2 tablespoons extra-virgin olive oil
8. 1 tablespoon lemon juice
9. Salt and pepper to taste
10. Lettuce leaves for serving

DIRECTIONS

1. In a bowl, mix together tuna, cucumber, red onion, bell peppers, olives, parsley, olive oil, lemon juice, salt, and pepper.

2. Spoon the tuna salad onto lettuce leaves.

3. Serve chilled.

Greek Zucchini Boats

Calories: 280 calories.   **Prep Time: 25 minutes.**

Servings: 2

INGREDIENTS

1. 2 large zucchini
2. 1/2 lb ground lamb or beef
3. 1/4 cup diced tomatoes
4. 1/4 cup diced red onion
5. 1/4 cup crumbled feta cheese
6. 2 tablespoons chopped fresh mint
7. 1 tablespoon olive oil
8. Salt and pepper to taste

DIRECTIONS

1. Preheat the oven to 375°F (190°C).

2. Cut the zucchini in half lengthwise, then scoop out the seeds to create boats.

3. In a skillet, cook ground lamb or beef over medium heat until browned and cooked through.

4. In a bowl, mix together cooked meat, diced tomatoes, red onion, feta cheese, mint, olive oil, salt, and pepper.

5. Spoon the mixture into the zucchini boats.

6. Place the zucchini boats in a baking dish and bake for 20-25 minutes, or until the zucchini is tender.

7. Serve hot.

Lemon Garlic Shrimp with Cauliflower Rice

Calories: 220 calories   **Prep Time: 15 minutes.**

Servings: 2

INGREDIENTS

1. 1 lb shrimp, peeled and deveined
2. 2 cups cauliflower rice
3. 2 cloves garlic, minced
4. 1 tablespoon olive oil
5. 1 tablespoon lemon juice
6. 1 tablespoon chopped fresh parsley
7. Salt and pepper to taste

DIRECTIONS

1 In a medium-size pan, heat the olive oil. Add the minced garlic and sauté until fragrant.

2. Add shrimp to the skillet and cook until pink and opaque.

3. Stir in cauliflower rice and cook until heated through.

4. Remove from heat and stir in lemon juice, parsley, salt, and pepper.

5. Serve hot.

Mediterranean Eggplant and Chickpea Salad

Calories: 250 calories   **Prep Time: 30 minutes**

Servings: 2

INGREDIENTS

1. 1 large eggplant, cubed
2. 1 can (15 oz) chickpeas, drained and rinsed
3. 1/4 cup diced red onion
4. 1/4 cup chopped fresh parsley
5. 2 tablespoons extra-virgin olive oil
6. 1 tablespoon balsamic vinegar
7. Salt and pepper to taste

DIRECTIONS

1. Preheat the oven to 400°F (200°C).

2. Spread the cubed eggplant on a baking sheet and drizzle with olive oil. Season with salt and pepper.

3. Roast in the preheated oven for 20-25 minutes, or until the eggplant is tender and golden brown.

4. In a large bowl, combine roasted eggplant, chickpeas, diced red onion, and chopped parsley.

5. Drizzle with extra-virgin olive oil and balsamic vinegar.

6. Toss gently to coat everything evenly.

7. Serve at room temperature.

Satisfying Dinners for Every Palate

Dinner Recipes That Don't Compromise on Nutrition!

Good evening, dinner-lovers! Dinner is a time to unwind and enjoy delicious cuisine. We'll uncover some delicious supper recipes that everyone will like.

Days	Recipes	Prep Time (Minutes)	Colories	Servings
Day 1	Lemon Herb Baked Salmon	20	300	2
Day 2	Mediterranean Cauliflower Rice Stir-Fry	20	250	2
Day 3	Greek Chicken Souvlaki Skewers	40	280	2
Day 4	Mediterranean Stuffed Portobello Mushroom	25	220	2
Day 5	Greek Lemon Chicken Soup (Avgolemono)	15	200	2
Day 6	Mediterranean Baked Cod with Tomato and Olive Relish	25	250	2
Day 7	Mediterranean Grilled Vegetable Platter	15	200	2

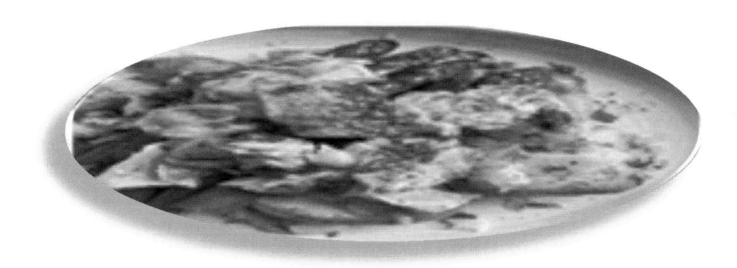

Lemon Herb Baked Salmon

Calories: 300 calories.   **Prep Time: 20 minutes**

Servings: 2

INGREDIENTS

1. 2 salmon fillets
2. 1 lemon, sliced
3. 2 cloves garlic, minced
4. 1 tablespoon chopped fresh dill
5. 1 tablespoon chopped fresh parsley
6. Salt and pepper to taste
7. 1 tablespoon olive oil

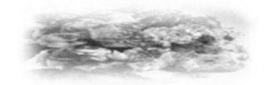

DIRECTIONS

1. Preheat the oven to 375°F (190°C).

2. Arrange the salmon fillets on a baking pan lined with parchment paper.

3. Season with minced garlic, chopped dill, chopped parsley, salt, and pepper.

4. Drizzle with olive oil and top with lemon slices.

5. Bake in the preheated oven for 12-15 minutes, or until the salmon is cooked through and flakes easily with a fork.

6. Serve hot.

Mediterranean Cauliflower Rice Stir-Fry

Calories: 250 calories   **Prep Time: 20 minutes**

Servings: 2

INGREDIENTS

1. 2 cups cauliflower rice
2. 1/2 lb cooked shrimp or chicken, diced
3. 1/4 cup diced bell peppers
4. 1/4 cup diced zucchini
5. 1/4 cup diced tomatoes
6. 2 cloves garlic, minced
7. 2 tablespoons chopped fresh parsley
8. 2 tablespoons extra-virgin olive oil
9. Salt and pepper to taste

DIRECTIONS

1. In a medium-size pan, heat the olive oil. Add the minced garlic and sauté until fragrant.

2. Add cauliflower rice, diced bell peppers, diced zucchini, and diced tomatoes to the skillet. Cook until vegetables are tender.

3. Stir in cooked shrimp or chicken and chopped parsley. Cook until heated through.

4. Season with salt and pepper to taste.

5. Serve hot.

Greek Chicken Souvlaki Skewers

Calories: 280 calories

Prep Time: 40 minutes

Servings: 2

INGREDIENTS

1. 2 chicken breasts, cut into cubes
2. 1/4 cup Greek yogurt
3. 1 tablespoon lemon juice
4. 1 tablespoon olive oil
5. 2 cloves garlic, minced
6. 1 teaspoon dried oregano
7. Salt and pepper to taste
8. Wooden skewers, soaked in water

DIRECTIONS

1. In a bowl, combine Greek yogurt, lemon juice, olive oil, minced garlic, dried oregano, salt, and pepper to make the marinade.

2. Toss the chicken cubes in the marinade until evenly coated. Cover and chill for at least 30 minutes.

3. Preheat the grill or grill pan to medium heat.

4. Thread the marinated chicken cubes onto wooden skewers.

5. Grill the skewers for 8-10 minutes, rotating regularly, until the chicken is well cooked and gently browned.

6. Serve hot.

Mediterranean Stuffed Portobello Mushroom

Calories: 220 calories   **Prep Time: 25 minutes**

Servings: 2

INGREDIENTS

1. 2 large Portobello mushrooms
2. 1/2 lb ground turkey or beef
3. 1/4 cup diced tomatoes
4. 1/4 cup diced red onion
5. 1/4 cup chopped spinach
6. 2 tablespoons crumbled feta cheese
7. 1 tablespoon chopped fresh parsley
8. 1 tablespoon olive oil
9. Salt and pepper to taste

DIRECTIONS

1. Preheat the oven to 375°F (190°C).

2. Remove the Portobello mushrooms' stems and use a spoon to carefully scrape out the gills.

3. In a skillet, cook ground turkey or beef over medium heat until browned and cooked through.

4. In a bowl, mix together cooked meat, diced tomatoes, red onion, spinach, feta cheese, parsley, olive oil, salt, and pepper.

5. Spoon the mixture into the mushroom caps.

6. Place the stuffed mushrooms on a baking sheet and bake for 20-25 minutes, or until the mushrooms are tender.

7. Serve hot.

Greek Lemon Chicken Soup (Avgolemono)

Calories: 200 calories   **Prep Time: 15 minutes**

Servings: 2

INGREDIENTS

1. 2 cups chicken broth
2. 1 cooked chicken breast, shredded
3. 1/4 cup uncooked orzo pasta
4. 2 eggs
5. Juice of 1 lemon
6. Salt and pepper to taste
7. Chopped fresh dill for garnish

DIRECTIONS

1. In a saucepan, heat the chicken broth until it boils.

2. Add the orzo pasta and cook according to package instructions until tender.

3. Reduce the heat to low and add the shredded chicken to the broth.

4. In a bowl, whisk together the eggs and lemon juice until frothy.

5. Slowly pour the egg mixture into the hot broth while whisking continuously to avoid curdling.

6. Continue to cook for a few minutes until the soup thickens slightly.

7. Season with salt and pepper as desired.

8. Serve hot, garnished with chopped fresh dill.

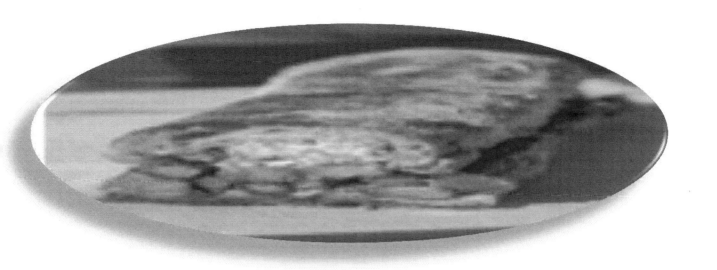

Mediterranean Baked Cod with Tomato and Olive Relish

Calories: 250 calories   **Prep Time: 25 minutes**

Servings: 2

INGREDIENTS

1. 2 cod fillets
2. 1 cup cherry tomatoes, halved
3. 1/4 cup Kalamata olives, pitted and chopped
4. 2 cloves garlic, minced
5. 2 tablespoons chopped fresh parsley
6. 1 tablespoon olive oil
7. Juice of 1 lemon
8. Salt and pepper to taste

DIRECTIONS

1. Preheat the oven to 375°F (190°C).

2. Put the fish fillets on a roasting tray.

3. In a bowl, mix together cherry tomatoes, chopped olives, minced garlic, chopped parsley, olive oil, lemon juice, salt, and pepper to make the relish.

4. Spoon the relish over the cod fillets.

5. Bake in the preheated oven for 15-20 minutes, or until the fish is cooked through and readily flaked with a fork.

6. Serve hot.

Mediterranean Grilled Vegetable Platter

Calories: 200 calories   **Prep Time: 15 minutes**

Servings: 2

INGREDIENTS

1. 1 small eggplant, sliced
2. 1 zucchini, sliced
3. 1 yellow squash, sliced
4. 1 red bell pepper, sliced
5. 1 red onion, sliced
6. 2 tablespoons olive oil
7. 2 cloves garlic, minced
8. 1 teaspoon dried oregano
9. Salt and pepper to taste

DIRECTIONS

1. Preheat the grill or grill pan over medium heat.

2. In a bowl, toss together the sliced vegetables with olive oil, minced garlic, dried oregano, salt, and pepper.

3. Grill the vegetables until tender and lightly charred, about 5-7 minutes per side.

4. Arrange the grilled vegetables on a platter.

5. Serve hot or at room temperature.

Snacks and Appetizers to Keep You Going

Hello, snack fans!

Sometimes we just need something to keep us going in between meals. Let's try some delicious snacks and appetizers to fulfil our hunger. Here are seven healthy Keto Mediterranean snack options for midday boosts targeted for you:

Days	Recipes	Prep Time (Minutes)	Colories	Servings
Day 1	Greek Yogurt with Honey and Walnuts	2	200	1
Day 2	Caprese Skewers	5	150	1
Day 3	Mediterranean Hummus Platter	5	180	1
Day 4	Stuffed Mini Bell Peppers	10	220	1
Day 5	Tzatziki with Veggie Sticks	5	100	1
Day 6	Mediterranean Antipasto Plate	5	250	1
Day 7	Greek Salad Cups	10	150	1

Greek Yogurt with Honey and Walnuts

Calories: 200 calories.   **Prep Time: 2 minutes.**

Servings: 1

INGREDIENTS

1. 1/2 cup Greek yogurt
2. 1 tablespoon honey
3. 1 tablespoon chopped walnuts

DIRECTIONS

1. In a bowl, spoon Greek yogurt.
2. Drizzle with honey.
3. Sprinkle chopped walnuts on top.
4. Serve chilled.

HEALTH BENEFITS

Rich in probiotics, protein, and healthy fats. Supports gut health, provides energy, and helps maintain muscle mass.

Caprese Skewers

Calories: 150 calories.   **Prep Time: 5 minutes.**

Servings: 1

INGREDIENTS

1. 4 cherry tomatoes
2. 4 small fresh mozzarella balls
3. 4 fresh basil leaves
4. 1 tablespoon balsamic glaze

HEALTH BENEFITS

Rich in antioxidants, vitamins, and minerals. Supports heart health, provides energy, and helps maintain bone density.

DIRECTIONS

1. Thread cherry tomatoes, mozzarella balls, and basil leaves onto skewers.
2. Drizzle with balsamic glaze.
3. Serve immediately.

Mediterranean Hummus Platter

Calories: 180 calories.   **Prep Time: 5 minutes.**

Servings: 1

INGREDIENTS

1. 1/4 cup hummus
2. 1 small cucumber, sliced
3. 1 small carrot, sliced
4. 4 cherry tomatoes
5. 4 Kalamata olives
6. 2 whole grain crackers

HEALTH BENEFITS

It is Rich in fiber, protein, and healthy fats. Supports digestion, provides energy, and helps maintain brain health.

DIRECTIONS

1. Spread hummus on a plate.

2. Arrange cucumber slices, carrot slices, cherry tomatoes, and Kalamata olives around the hummus.

3. Serve with whole grain crackers.

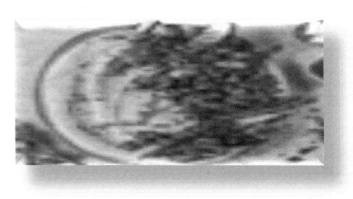

Stuffed Mini Bell Peppers

Calories: 220 calories.   **Prep Time: 10 minutes.**

Servings: 1

INGREDIENTS

1. 4 mini bell peppers
2. 2 tablespoons whipped cream cheese
3. 2 tablespoons diced cucumber
4. 2 tablespoons diced tomatoes
5. 1 tablespoon chopped fresh parsley

HEALTH BENEFITS

Rich in vitamins, minerals, and antioxidants. Supports immune health, provides energy, and helps maintain eye health.

DIRECTIONS

1. 1. Slice the tops off the mini bell peppers and remove the seeds.

2. In a bowl, mix together whipped cream cheese, diced cucumber, diced tomatoes, and chopped fresh parsley.

3. Stuff the mixture into the mini bell peppers.

4. Serve chilled or at room temperature.

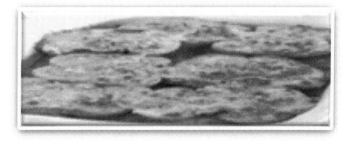

Tzatziki with Veggie Sticks

Calories: 100 calories.   **Prep Time: 5 minutes.**

Servings: 1

INGREDIENTS

1. 1/4 cup Greek yogurt
2. 1/4 cup grated cucumber
3. 1 clove garlic, minced
4. 1 tablespoon chopped fresh dill
5. 1 tablespoon lemon juice
6. Salt and pepper to taste
7. Assorted veggie sticks (carrots, celery, bell peppers)

DIRECTIONS

1. In a bowl, combine Greek yogurt, grated cucumber, minced garlic, chopped fresh dill, lemon juice, salt, and pepper to make the tzatziki sauce.

2. Serve the tzatziki sauce with assorted veggie sticks.

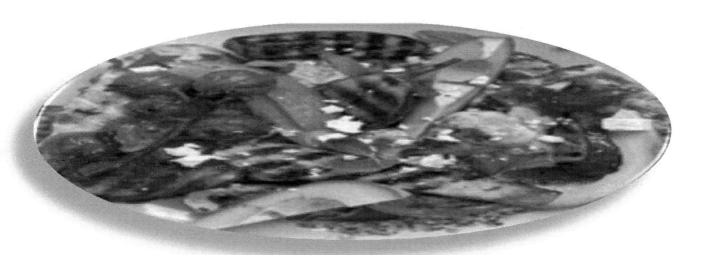

Mediterranean Antipasto Plate

Calories: 250 calories.   **Prep Time: 5 minutes.**

Servings: 1

INGREDIENTS

1. 2 slices prosciutto
2. 2 slices salami
3. 2 slices provolone cheese
4. 1/4 cup marinated artichoke hearts
5. 1/4 cup roasted red peppers
6. 2 tablespoons mixed olives
7. 2 whole grain crackers

DIRECTIONS

1. Arrange prosciutto, salami, provolone cheese, marinated artichoke hearts, roasted red peppers and mixed olives on a plate.

2. Serve with whole grain crackers on the side.

Greek Salad Cups

Calories: 150 calories.   **Prep Time: 10 minutes.**

Servings: 1

INGREDIENTS

1. 1/2 cup diced cucumber
2. 1/2 cup diced tomatoes
3. 1/4 cup diced red onion
4. 1/4 cup crumbled feta cheese
5. 2 tablespoons Kalamata olives, chopped
6. 1 tablespoon extra-virgin olive oil
7. 1 tablespoon lemon juice
8. Salt and pepper to taste
9. Lettuce leaves for serving

DIRECTIONS

1. In a bowl, combine diced cucumber, diced tomatoes, diced red onion, crumbled feta cheese, and chopped Kalamata olives.
2. Drizzle with extra-virgin olive oil and lemon juice.
3. Add salt and pepper to taste.
4. Spoon the salad mixture into lettuce leaves to form cups.
5. Serve chilled.

Sides and Salads to Complete Your Meals

Vibrant Side Dish Recipes Featuring Fresh Produce!

Adding sides and salads to our meals enhances their flavor. We'll learn about some simple and delicious side dishes that complement our entrees. Here are seven bright Keto Mediterranean side dish dishes with fresh fruit for seniors:

Days	Recipes	Prep Time (Minutes)	Colories	Servings
Day 1	Roasted Garlic and Herb Cauliflower Mash	35	100	2
Day 2	Greek Cucumber Salad	10	120	2
Day 3	Lemon Garlic Roasted Brussels Sprouts	30	100	2
Day 4	Mediterranean Grilled Eggplant	15	120	2
Day 5	Greek Stuffed Tomatoes (Gemista)	40	180	2
Day 6	Lemon Garlic Roasted Asparagus	15	80	2
Day 7	Mediterranean Roasted Vegetable Platter	20	150	2

Roasted Garlic and Herb Cauliflower Mash

Calories: 100 calories.   **Prep Time: 35 minutes.**

Servings: 2

INGREDIENTS

1. 1 head cauliflower, cut into florets
2. 2 cloves garlic, minced
3. 2 tablespoons olive oil
4. 1 tablespoon chopped fresh thyme
5. Salt and pepper to taste

DIRECTIONS

1. Whisk eggs in a bowl and season with salt and pepper.
2. Heat olive oil in a skillet over medium heat.
3. Add tomatoes, spinach, and bell peppers, sauté until tender.
4. Pour eggs into the skillet, cook until set.
5. Fold omelette and serve hot.

Greek Cucumber Salad

Calories: 120 calories.   **Prep Time: 10 minutes.**

Servings: 2

INGREDIENTS

1. 1 English cucumber, sliced
2. 1/4 cup diced red onion
3. 1/4 cup cherry tomatoes, halved
4. 2 tablespoons chopped Kalamata olives
5. 2 tablespoons crumbled feta cheese
6. 2 tablespoons extra-virgin olive oil
7. 1 tablespoon red wine vinegar
8. 1 tablespoon chopped fresh parsley
9. Salt and pepper to taste

DIRECTIONS

1. In a bowl, combine sliced cucumber, diced red onion, cherry tomatoes, Kalamata olives, and crumbled feta cheese.

2. In a small bowl, whisk together extra-virgin olive oil, red wine vinegar, chopped parsley, salt, and pepper to make the dressing.

3. Drizzle the dressing over the salad and gently toss to blend.

4. Serve chilled.

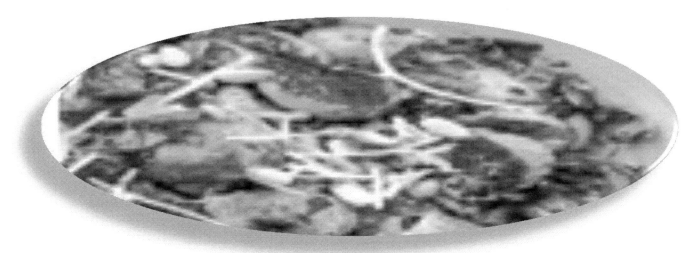

Lemon Garlic Roasted Brussels Sprouts

Calories: 100 calories.   **Prep Time: 30 minutes.**

Servings: 2

INGREDIENTS

1. 1/2 lb Brussels sprouts, trimmed and halved
2. 2 cloves garlic, minced
3. 2 tablespoons olive oil
4. 1 tablespoon lemon juice
5. 1 teaspoon lemon zest
6. Salt and pepper to taste

DIRECTIONS

1. Preheat the oven to 400°F (200°C).

2. Toss Brussels sprouts and minced garlic with olive oil, lemon juice, lemon zest, salt, and pepper.

3. Spread the mixture on a baking sheet lined with parchment paper.

4. Roast in the preheated oven for 20-25 minutes, or until Brussels sprouts are tender and caramelized.

5. Serve hot.

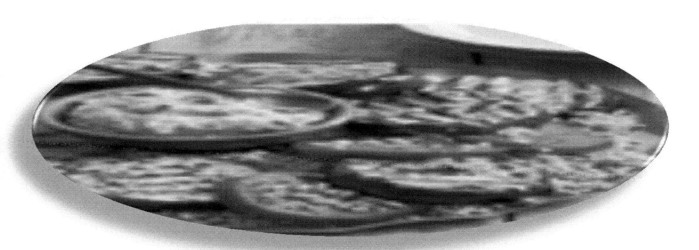

Mediterranean Grilled Eggplant

Calories: 120 calories.   **Prep Time: 15 minutes.**

Servings: 2

INGREDIENTS

1. 1 large eggplant, sliced into rounds
2. 2 tablespoons extra-virgin olive oil
3. 1 tablespoon balsamic vinegar
4. 1 teaspoon dried oregano
5. Salt and pepper to taste

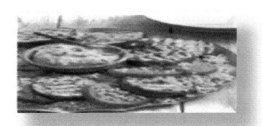

DIRECTIONS

1. Preheat the grill or grill pan over medium heat.

2. In a bowl, whisk together extra-virgin olive oil, balsamic vinegar, dried oregano, salt, and pepper.

3. Brush the olive oil mixture onto both sides of the eggplant pieces.

4. Grill the eggplant slices for 3-4 minutes per side, or until tender and grill marks appear.

5. Serve hot or at room temperature.

Greek Stuffed Tomatoes (Gemista)

Calories: 180 calories.   **Prep Time: 40 minutes.**

Servings: 2

INGREDIENTS

1. 2 large beefsteak tomatoes
2. 1/2 cup cooked quinoa
3. 1/4 cup diced cucumber
4. 1/4 cup diced red onion
5. 1/4 cup chopped fresh parsley
6. 2 tablespoons crumbled feta cheese
7. 2 tablespoons extra-virgin olive oil
8. 1 tablespoon red wine vinegar
9. Salt and pepper to taste

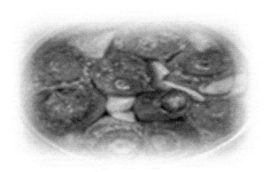

DIRECTIONS

1. Preheat the oven to 375°F (190°C).

2. Slice the tops off the tomatoes and carefully scoop out the seeds and pulp to create a hollow cavity.

3. In a bowl, mix together cooked quinoa, diced cucumber, diced red onion, chopped parsley, crumbled feta cheese, extra-virgin olive oil, red wine vinegar, salt, and pepper.

4. Stuff the quinoa mixture into the hollowed-out tomatoes.

5. Place the stuffed tomatoes in a baking dish and bake in the preheated oven for 20-25 minutes, or until tomatoes are tender.

6. Serve hot.

Lemon Garlic Roasted Asparagus

Calories: 80 calories.   **Prep Time: 15 minutes.**

Servings: 2

INGREDIENTS

1. 1/2 lb asparagus spears, trimmed
2. 2 cloves garlic, minced
3. 2 tablespoons extra-virgin olive oil
4. 1 tablespoon lemon juice
5. 1 teaspoon lemon zest
6. Salt and pepper to taste

DIRECTIONS

11. Preheat the oven to 400°F (200°C).
2. Toss asparagus spears and minced garlic with extra-virgin olive oil, lemon juice, lemon zest, salt, and pepper.
3. Spread the asparagus on a baking sheet lined with parchment paper.
4. Roast in the preheated oven for 10-12 minutes, or until asparagus is tender and lightly browned.
5. Serve hot.

Mediterranean Roasted Vegetable Platter

Calories: 150 calories.   **Prep Time: 30 minutes.**

Servings: 2

INGREDIENTS

1. 1 red bell pepper, sliced
2. 1 yellow bell pepper, sliced
3. 1 zucchini, sliced
4. 1 yellow squash, sliced
5. 1 red onion, sliced
6. 2 tablespoons extra-virgin olive oil
7. 1 tablespoon balsamic vinegar
8. 1 teaspoon dried Italian herbs
9. Salt and pepper to taste

DIRECTIONS

1. Preheat the oven to 400°F (200°C).

2. Toss sliced bell peppers, zucchini, yellow squash, and red onion with extra-virgin olive oil, balsamic vinegar, dried Italian herbs , salt, and pepper.

3. Spread the vegetables on a baking sheet lined with parchment paper.

4. Roast in the preheated oven for 20-25 minutes, or until the vegetables are tender and caramelized.

5. Serve hot or at room temperature.

Guilt-Free Dessert Recipes for Sweet Tooth Satisfaction!

Sweet tooth alert! Who doesn't enjoy dessert? Let's look at some tasty and nutritious dessert alternatives that we may eat guilt-free. Here are seven guilt-free keto Mediterranean dessert dishes designed specifically for you:

Days	Recipes	Prep Time (Minutes)	Colories	Servings
Day 1	Greek Yogurt with Berries and Honey	30 :	380	2
Day 2	Almond Flour Lemon Poppy Seed Muffins	30	150	2
Day 3	Coconut Chia Pudding	5	150	2
Day 4	Baked Cinnamon Apple Slices	10	100	2
Day 5	Dark Chocolate Avocado Mousse	30	150	2
Day 6	Berry Greek Yogurt Popsicles	5	50	4
Day 7	Coconut Flour Lemon Bars	10	90	8

Greek Yogurt with Berries and Honey

Calories: 380 calories.   **Prep Time: 30 minutes.**

Servings: 2

INGREDIENTS

1. 1/2 cup Greek yogurt
2. 1/4 cup mixed berries (such as raspberries, blueberries, and strawberries)
3. 1 tablespoon honey

DIRECTIONS

1. In a bowl, spoon Greek yogurt.
2. Top with mixed berries.
3. Drizzle with honey.
4. Serve chilled.

Almond Flour Lemon Poppy Seed Muffins

Calories: 150 calories.   **Prep Time: 30 minutes.**

Servings: 2

INGREDIENTS

1. 1 cup almond flour
2. 2 tablespoons coconut flour
3. 2 tablespoons erythritol (or preferred sweetener)
4. 1 teaspoon baking powder
5. 1/4 teaspoon salt
6. 2 tablespoons poppy seeds
7. Zest of 1 lemon
8. 2 large eggs
9. 1/4 cup unsweetened almond milk
10. 1/4 cup melted coconut oil
11. 1 teaspoon vanilla extract
12. Juice of 1 lemon

DIRECTIONS

1 Preheat the oven to 350°F (175°C). Line the muffin tray with paper liners.

2. In a large bowl, whisk together almond flour, coconut flour, erythritol, baking powder, salt, poppy seeds, and lemon zest.

3. In another bowl, whisk together eggs, almond milk, melted coconut oil, vanilla extract, and lemon juice.

4 Pour the wet ingredients into the dry ingredients and whisk until thoroughly blended.

5. Distribute the batter evenly between the muffin cups.

6. Place in the preheated oven for 18-20 minutes, or until a toothpick inserted in the center comes out clean.

7. Allow muffins to cool before serving.

Coconut Chia Pudding

Calories: 150 calories.   **Prep Time: 5 minutes.**

Servings: 2

INGREDIENTS

1. 1/4 cup chia seeds
2. 1 cup unsweetened coconut milk
3. 1 tablespoon erythritol (or preferred sweetener)
4. 1/2 teaspoon vanilla extract
5. Unsweetened shredded coconut for garnish

DIRECTIONS

1. In a bowl, whisk together chia seeds, coconut milk, erythritol, and vanilla extract.

2. Cover and refrigerate for at least 2 hours or overnight, until the mixture thickens and forms a pudding-like consistency.

3. Stir well before serving.

4. Garnish with unsweetened shredded coconut.

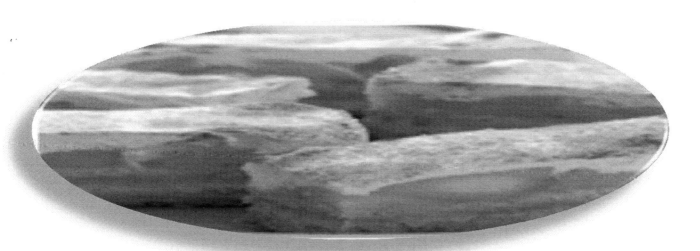

Baked Cinnamon Apple Slices

Calories: 100 calories.   **Prep Time: 10 minutes.**

Servings: 2

INGREDIENTS

1. 2 medium apples, cored and sliced
2. 1 tablespoon melted coconut oil
3. 1 teaspoon ground cinnamon
4. 1/2 teaspoon ground nutmeg
5. 1/4 teaspoon ground cloves
6. 1 tablespoon erythritol (or preferred sweetener)

DIRECTIONS

1. Preheat the oven to 375°F (190°C). Line a baking sheet with parchment paper.

2. In a bowl, toss apple slices with melted coconut oil, ground cinnamon, ground nutmeg, ground cloves, and erythritol.

3. Spread the apple slices in a single layer on the prepared baking sheet.

4. Bake in the preheated oven for 20-25 minutes, or until apples are tender and lightly caramelized.

5. Serve warm.

Dark Chocolate Avocado Mousse

Calories: 150 calories.   **Prep Time: 30 minutes.**

Servings: 2

INGREDIENTS

1. 1 ripe avocado
2. 2 tablespoons unsweetened cocoa powder
3. 2 tablespoons powdered erythritol (or preferred sweetener)
4. 1/2 teaspoon vanilla extract
5. Pinch of salt
6. Unsweetened almond milk (as needed for consistency)
7. Dark chocolate shavings for garnish

DIRECTIONS

1. Scoop the flesh of the avocado into a food processor.

2. Combine the cocoa powder, powdered erythritol, vanilla essence, and a sprinkle of salt.

3. Blend until smooth, adding almond milk as needed to achieve a creamy consistency.

4. Divide the mousse into serving bowls.

5. Garnish with dark chocolate shavings.

6. Serve chilled.

Berry Greek Yogurt Popsicles

Calories: 50 calories.   **Prep Time: 5 minutes.**

Servings: 4

INGREDIENTS

1. 1 cup Greek yogurt
2. 1/4 cup mixed berries (like strawberries, blueberries, and raspberries)
3. 1 tablespoon honey or erythritol (optional)

DIRECTIONS

1. In a blender, combine Greek yogurt, mixed berries, and honey or erythritol (if using).

2. Blend until smooth.

3. Pour the mixture into popsicle molds.

4. Insert popsicle sticks into the molds.

5. Freeze for at least 4 hours, or until fully frozen.

6. To remove the popsicles from the molds, run warm water over the outside of the molds for a few seconds.

7. Serve immediately.

Coconut Flour Lemon Bars

Calories: 90 calories.　　　　**Prep Time: 10 minutes.**

Servings: 8

INGREDIENTS

1. 1/2 cup coconut flour
2. 1/4 cup melted coconut oil
3. 2 tablespoons powdered erythritol (or preferred sweetener)
4. 3 large eggs
5. Zest of 1 lemon
6. Juice of 1 lemon
7. 1/4 teaspoon baking powder
8. Pinch of salt

DIRECTIONS

1. Preheat the oven to 350°F (175°C).

2. Line an 8x8-inch baking dish with parchment paper, allowing some overhang on each side.

3. In a bowl, mix together coconut flour, melted coconut oil, powdered erythritol, eggs, lemon zest, lemon juice, baking powder, and a pinch of salt until well combined.

4. Press the mixture into the bottom of the prepared baking dish in an even layer.

5. Bake in a preheated oven for 12-15 minutes, or until the edges are gently brown.

6. Remove from the oven and let it cool completely in the pan.

7. Once cooled, lift the parchment paper to remove the bars from the pan and transfer to a cutting board.

8. Cut into squares or bars.

9. Serve chilled.

Special Occasion and Holiday Favourites

festive Recipes to Celebrate Holidays and Special Occasions!

Hello, party planners! Holidays and special events are ideal opportunities to enjoy with delicious meals. We will offer some favorite dishes that are ideal for these special occasions. Below are seven simple keto Mediterranean festive meals ideal for seniors to celebrate holidays and special events.

Days	Recipes	Prep Time (Minutes)	Colories	Servings
Day 1	Herb-Roasted Turkey Breast	10	250	4
Day 2	Cauliflower and Broccoli Gratin	20	200	6
Day 3	Grilled Lemon Garlic Shrimp Skewers	30	150	4
Day 4	Mediterranean Stuffed Bell Peppers	20	300	4
Day 5	Eggplant Involtini	20	250	4
Day 6	Greek Lamb Meatballs with Tzatziki Sauce	20	300	4
Day 7	Mediterranean Stuffed Zucchini Boats	20	200	4

Herb-Roasted Turkey Breast

Calories: 250 calories.   **Prep Time: 10 minutes.**

Servings: 4

INGREDIENTS

1. 1 bone-in turkey breast (about 4 pounds)
2. 2 tablespoons olive oil
3. 2 cloves garlic, minced
4. 1 tablespoon chopped fresh rosemary
5. 1 tablespoon chopped fresh thyme
6. 1 tablespoon chopped fresh sage
7. Salt and pepper to taste

DIRECTIONS

1. Preheat the oven to 375°F (190°C).

2. In a small bowl, mix together olive oil, minced garlic, chopped rosemary, thyme, sage, salt, and pepper.

3. Put the turkey breast in a roasting pan.

4. Apply the herb mixture all over the turkey breast.

5. Roast in the preheated oven for 1.5-2 hours, or until the internal temperature reaches 165°F (75°C) and the skin is golden brown.

6. Let the turkey breast rest for 10-15 minutes before slicing.

7. Serve hot.

Cauliflower and Broccoli Gratin

Calories: 200 calories.

Prep Time: 20 minutes.

Servings: 6

1. 1 head cauliflower, cut into florets
2. 1 head broccoli, cut into florets
3. 2 tablespoons olive oil
4. 2 cloves garlic, minced
5. 1 cup heavy cream
6. 1 cup shredded mozzarella cheese
7. 1/4 cup grated Parmesan cheese
8. Salt and pepper to taste
9. Chopped fresh parsley for garnish

DIRECTIONS

1. Preheat the oven to 375°F (190°C).

2. In a large pot of salted boiling water, blanch cauliflower and broccoli florets for 2-3 minutes. Drain and set aside.

3. In a saucepan, heat the olive oil over medium heat. Add the minced garlic and cook until fragrant.

4. Stir in the heavy cream, mozzarella, and Parmesan cheese. Cook until the cheese melts and the sauce is smooth.

5. Season with salt and pepper to taste.

6. Arrange blanched cauliflower and broccoli in a baking dish.

7. Pour the cheese sauce over the vegetables, making sure they are evenly coated.

8. Bake in the preheated oven for 20-25 minutes, or until the gratin is bubbly and golden brown.

9. Before serving, garnish with finely chopped fresh parsley.

Grilled Lemon Garlic Shrimp Skewers

Calories: 150 calories.

Prep Time: 30 minutes.

Servings: 4

INGREDIENTS

1. 1 lb large shrimp, peeled and deveined
2. 2 tablespoons olive oil
3. 2 cloves garlic, minced
4. Zest and juice of 1 lemon
5. 1 tablespoon chopped fresh parsley
6. Salt and pepper to taste
7. Wooden skewers, soaked in water for 30 minutes

DIRECTIONS

1. Preheat the grill or grill pan to medium-high heat.

2. In a bowl, mix together olive oil, minced garlic, lemon zest, lemon juice, chopped parsley, salt, and pepper.

3. Add the shrimp to the bowl and toss to coat evenly.

4. Thread the shrimp on the moistened wooden skewers.

5. Grill the shrimp skewers for 2-3 minutes per side, or until the shrimp are opaque and lightly charred.

6. Remove from the grill and serve immediately.

Mediterranean Stuffed Bell Peppers

Calories: 300 calories.

Prep Time: 20 minutes.

Servings: 4

INGREDIENTS

1. 4 large bell peppers, halved and seeds removed
2. 1 lb ground turkey or chicken
3. 1 tablespoon olive oil
4. 1 small onion, diced
5. 2 cloves garlic, minced
6. 1 cup cauliflower rice
7. 1 cup diced tomatoes

CONTINUE NEXT PAGE....

DIRECTIONS

1. Preheat the oven to 375°F (190°C).

2. In a pan, heat the olive oil over medium heat. Sauté sliced onion and minced garlic until tender.

3. Add ground turkey or chicken to the skillet and cook until browned.

4. Stir in cauliflower rice, diced tomatoes, chopped parsley, dried oregano, smoked paprika, salt, and pepper. Cook for another 5 minutes.

5. Arrange bell pepper halves in a baking dish.

6. Spoon the turkey or chicken mixture into each bell pepper half.

Mediterranean Stuffed Bell Peppers

Calories: 300 calories.   **Prep Time: 20 minutes.**

Servings: 4

INGREDIENTS

8. 1/4 cup chopped fresh parsley
9. 1 teaspoon dried oregano
10. 1/2 teaspoon smoked paprika
11. Salt and pepper to taste
12. 1/2 cup shredded mozzarella cheese (optional)
13. Chopped fresh basil for garnish

DIRECTIONS

7. If using, sprinkle shredded mozzarella cheese over the stuffed peppers.

8. Cover the baking dish with aluminum foil and bake for 30-35 minutes, or until the peppers are soft.

9. Remove the foil and bake for an additional 5 minutes to melt the cheese (if using).

10. Garnish with chopped fresh basil before serving

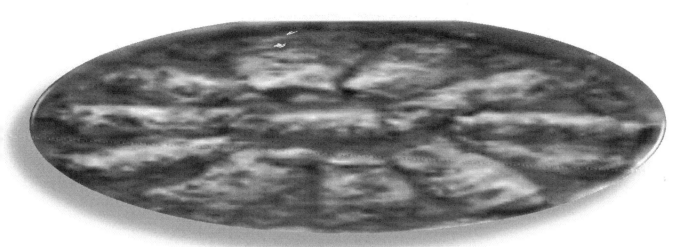

Eggplant Involtini

Calories: 250 calories.   **Prep Time: 20 minutes.**

Servings: 4

INGREDIENTS

1. 1 large eggplant, sliced lengthwise into thin strips
2. 2 tablespoons olive oil
3. Salt and pepper to taste
4. 1 cup ricotta cheese
5. 1/4 cup grated Parmesan cheese
6. 1/4 cup chopped fresh basil
7. 1 cup marinara sauce
8. 1/4 cup shredded mozzarella cheese
9. Chopped fresh parsley for garnish

DIRECTIONS

1. Preheat the oven to 375°F (190°C).

2. Brush olive oil onto eggplant slices and season with salt and pepper.

3. Heat a grill pan or skillet over medium heat. Grill the eggplant slices for 2-3 minutes per side, or until tender and grill marks appear. Set aside.

4. In a bowl, combine ricotta cheese, grated Parmesan cheese, and chopped fresh basil.

5. Spread a spoonful of marinara sauce on each grilled eggplant slice.

Eggplant Involtini

Calories: 250 calories.   **Prep Time: 30 minutes.**

Servings: 2

INGREDIENTS

Eggplant Involtini

Continuation...

DIRECTIONS

6. Place a dollop of the ricotta mixture at one end of each eggplant slice and roll up tightly.

7. Arrange the eggplant rolls in a baking dish, seam side down.

8. Spoon the remaining marinara sauce over the eggplant rolls.

9. Sprinkle shredded mozzarella cheese over the top.

10. Cover the baking dish with aluminum foil and bake in the preheated oven for 20-25 minutes, or until the cheese is melted and bubbly.

11. Remove the foil and bake for an additional 5 minutes to brown the cheese.

12. Garnish with chopped fresh parsley before serving.

Greek Lamb Meatballs with Tzatziki Sauce

Calories: 300 calories.   **Prep Time: 20 minutes.**

Servings: 4

Ingredients for Lamb Meatballs

1. 1 lb ground lamb
2. 1/4 cup almond flour
3. 1 small onion, grated
4. 2 cloves garlic, minced
5. 1 tablespoon chopped fresh mint
6. 1 tablespoon chopped fresh parsley
7. 1 teaspoon ground cumin
8. 1 teaspoon ground coriander
9. Salt and pepper to taste
10. Olive oil for frying

Preparation Instructions for Lamb Meatballs

1. In a bowl, combine ground lamb, almond flour, grated onion, minced garlic, chopped mint, chopped parsley, ground cumin, ground coriander, salt, and pepper. Mix until well combined.

2. Shape the mixture into small meatballs.

3. In a medium-size pan, heat the olive oil. Fry the meatballs in batches until browned on both sides and cooked through, 8-10 minutes.

4. Remove from the skillet and drain on paper towels.

Greek Lamb Meatballs with Tzatziki Sauce

Calories: 300 calories.　　　**Prep Time: 20 minutes.**

Servings: 4

Ingredients for Tzatziki Sauce

1. 1 cup Greek yogurt
2. 1/2 cucumber, grated and squeezed to remove excess liquid
3. 1 clove garlic, minced
4. 1 tablespoon chopped fresh dill
5. 1 tablespoon lemon juice
6. Salt and pepper to taste

Preparation Instructions for Tzatziki Sauce:

1. In a bowl, combine Greek yogurt, grated cucumber, minced garlic, chopped dill, lemon juice, salt, and pepper. Mix until well combined.

2. Refrigerate the tzatziki sauce for at least 30 minutes to allow the flavors to meld.

ASSEMBLY

1. Serve the Greek lamb meatballs hot with the chilled tzatziki sauce on the side.

2. Garnish with additional chopped fresh mint and parsley if desired.

Prep time: 20 minutes | cooking time: 20 minutes | chilling time: 30 minutes

Mediterranean Stuffed Zucchini Boats

Calories: 200 calories.   **Prep Time: 20 minutes.**

Servings: 4

INGREDIENTS

1. 2 large zucchini
2. 1 tablespoon olive oil
3. 1 small onion, diced
4. 2 cloves garlic, minced
5. 1 bell pepper, diced
6. 1 cup diced tomatoes
7. 1/2 cup cooked quinoa
8. 1/4 cup chopped fresh parsley
9. 1 teaspoon dried oregano
10. 1/2 teaspoon smoked paprika
11. Salt and pepper to taste
12. 1/4 cup crumbled feta cheese
13. Chopped fresh basil for garnish

DIRECTIONS

1. Preheat the oven to 375°F (190°C).

2. Cut the zucchini in half lengthwise and scoop out the flesh to create a hollow boat shape. Set aside.

3. In a pan, heat the olive oil over medium heat. Sauté sliced onion and minced garlic until tender.

4. Add diced bell pepper to the skillet and cook until softened.

5. Stir in diced tomatoes, cooked quinoa, chopped parsley, dried oregano, smoked paprika, salt, and pepper. Cook for another 5 minutes.

Mediterranean Stuffed Zucchini Boats

Calories: 200 calories.   **Prep Time: 20 minutes.**

Servings: 4

INGREDIENTS

DIRECTIONS

Mediterranean Stuffed Zucchini Boats

Continuation…..

6. Spoon the quinoa mixture into the hollowed-out zucchini boats.

7. Sprinkle crumbled feta cheese over the top of each zucchini boat.

8. Place the stuffed zucchini boats in a baking dish.

9. Cover the baking dish with aluminum foil and bake in the preheated oven for 25-30 minutes, or until the zucchini is tender.

10. Remove the foil and bake for an additional 5 minutes to melt the cheese.

11. Garnish with chopped fresh basil before serving.

Prep Time: 20 minutes | Cooking Time: 30-35 minutes

Chapter

Staying Active and Healthy Beyond the Kitchen

Being healthy requires more than simply eating well. Let's speak about remaining active and feeling well in all parts of life. As we approach our elderly years, keeping an active lifestyle becomes increasingly important for our general health and well-being. Physical activity is not only good for preserving mobility and independence, but it also helps to avoid chronic diseases and promotes longevity. In this part, we'll look at the benefits of physical activity for seniors and practical strategies to include it into your regular routine.

1. Maintaining Mobility and Independence

Regular physical activity is key to preserving mobility and independence as we age. Engaging in activities that challenge balance, flexibility, strength, and endurance can help prevent falls and maintain functional abilities essential for performing daily tasks independently. Whether it's walking, swimming, yoga, or tai chi, finding activities that suit your interests and abilities is paramount to staying active and independent.

2. Preventing Chronic Diseases

Physical activity plays a significant role in reducing the risk of chronic diseases commonly associated with aging, such as heart disease, diabetes, osteoporosis, and certain types of cancer. Regular exercise helps control blood pressure, cholesterol levels, and blood sugar levels, thereby reducing the risk of cardiovascular disease and diabetes. Additionally, weight-bearing exercises help maintain bone density and muscle mass, lowering the risk of osteoporosis and frailty.

3. Enhancing Mental Well being

Exercise not only benefits physical health but also has a significant influence on mental well-being. Endorphins, neurotransmitters that enhance happiness while also reducing stress and anxiety, are released during physical exercise. Regular exercise has been related to enhanced cognitive function, memory, and mood, lowering the risk of cognitive decline and depression in older adults.

4. Improving Quality of Life

Staying physically active contributes to a higher quality of life in our later years. Engaging in regular exercise promotes better sleep, increases energy levels, and enhances overall vitality. It fosters a sense of accomplishment and empowerment, boosting self-esteem and confidence. Moreover, participating in group activities or exercise classes provides opportunities for social interaction and community engagement, reducing feelings of isolation and loneliness.

5. Longevity and Healthy Aging

Leading an active lifestyle is one of the key pillars of healthy aging and longevity. Research has consistently shown that regular physical activity is associated with a longer life expectancy and a lower risk of premature death. By adopting a balanced approach that includes both aerobic and strength-training exercises, you can optimize their physical health, maintain independence, and enjoy a fulfilling and active lifestyle well into their later years.

Gentle Exercises and Activities for Seniors

Morning and evening exercise into your routine is a powerful way to enhance your progress on the Keto Mediterranean Diet journey outlined in this book. I understand the importance of a holistic approach to health and well-being, which is why I've included comprehensive guidance on integrating physical activity seamlessly into your daily life.

Morning Exercise Routine

Starting your day with exercise sets a positive tone and energizes both your body and mind. Here's a practical morning exercise routine tailored for seniors:

1. Stretching: Begin with gentle stretching exercises to wake up your muscles and increase flexibility. Focus on movements that target major muscle groups, such as arm circles, leg swings, and neck rotations.

2. Cardiovascular Exercise: Engage in low-impact aerobic activities such as walking, cycling, or swimming. Aim for at least 20-30 minutes of moderate-intensity cardio to boost your heart health and metabolism.

3. Strength Training: Incorporate resistance exercises to build muscle strength and support joint health. Use light weights, resistance bands, or perform bodyweight exercises like squats, lunges, and modified push-ups.

4. Balance and Stability Work: Dedicate time to improve balance and stability through exercises like standing on one leg, heel-to-toe walking, or practicing yoga poses that focus on balance.

5. Mindfulness Practice: Conclude your morning routine with a brief mindfulness or meditation session to center yourself and set positive intentions for the day ahead.

Evening Exercise Routine

In the evening, exercise can help you unwind from the day's activities, promote relaxation, and prepare your body for restorative sleep. Here's a practical evening exercise routine for seniors:

1. Light Cardio: Take a leisurely stroll around your neighborhood or engage in gentle cycling to wind down from the day's events. Aim for 15-20 minutes of light cardiovascular activity to promote blood circulation and relaxation.

2. Yoga or Tai Chi: Practice gentle yoga or Tai Chi exercises to release tension, improve flexibility, and promote relaxation. Focus on gentle stretches, deep breathing, and mindful movement to calm the mind and body.

3. Foam Rolling: Use a foam roller to perform self-myofascial release techniques, targeting areas of tightness or discomfort in your muscles. Roll slowly over each muscle group, pausing on areas of tension to help release knots and improve mobility.

4. Deep Breathing Exercises: Incorporate deep breathing exercises or guided relaxation techniques to reduce stress and promote restful sleep. Practice diaphragmatic breathing or progressive muscle relaxation to quiet the mind and prepare for bedtime.

5. Bedtime Stretches: Finish your evening routine with gentle stretches designed to promote relaxation and improve sleep quality. Focus on stretches that target tight muscles, such as the hamstrings, hips, and shoulders, holding each stretch for 20-30 seconds.

Holistic Approaches to Wellness and Aging Gracefully

The holistic approaches to wellness is essential for aging gracefully and maintaining optimal health and vitality. While the keto Mediterranean diet serves as a cornerstone for promoting heart-healthy aging and weight loss, integrating holistic practices can further enhance your well-being on physical, mental, and emotional levels. In this section, we'll explore holistic approaches to wellness that complement the keto Mediterranean lifestyle and support aging gracefully.

1. Mindful Eating

Practicing mindful eating involves paying attention to the sensory experience of eating and being fully present during meals. By savoring each bite, chewing slowly, and tuning into hunger and fullness cues, you can develop a healthier relationship with food and prevent overeating. Mindful eating also encourages appreciation for the nourishing qualities of whole, nutrient-dense foods, aligning with the principles of the keto Mediterranean diet.

2. Stress Management

Chronic stress can have detrimental effects on overall health and well-being, contributing to inflammation, hormonal imbalances, and increased risk of chronic diseases. Implementing stress management techniques such as meditation, deep breathing exercises, yoga, and tai chi can help reduce stress levels, promote relaxation, and support mental clarity. These practices not only enhance your ability to cope with life's challenges but also contribute to a sense of inner peace and resilience.

3. Regular Movement and Exercise:

Physical activity is vital for maintaining mobility, strength, and flexibility as we age. Incorporating regular movement and exercise into your daily routine supports cardiovascular health, strengthens muscles and bones, and enhances overall vitality. Whether it's brisk walking, swimming, dancing, or practicing yoga, finding activities that you enjoy and that align with your fitness level is key to staying active and energized.

4. Adequate Sleep

Quality sleep is essential for optimal health and well-being, yet many seniors struggle with sleep disturbances and insomnia. Prioritizing sleep hygiene practices such as maintaining a consistent sleep schedule, creating a relaxing bedtime routine, and optimizing your sleep environment can improve sleep quality and duration. Adequate restorative sleep supports cognitive function, immune function, and overall resilience.

5. Social Connection

Maintaining social connections and fostering meaningful relationships is crucial for emotional well-being and mental health. Engaging in regular social activities, spending time with loved ones, and participating in community events can combat feelings of isolation and loneliness often experienced in older age. Cultivating a strong support network provides emotional support, companionship, and a sense of belonging.

6. Holistic Self Care

Self-care practices encompass a wide range of activities that nurture your physical, mental, and emotional well-being. This includes activities such as spending time in nature, practicing gratitude, indulging in hobbies and interests, and seeking professional support when needed. Taking time for self-care allows you to recharge, replenish your energy reserves, and cultivate a sense of balance and fulfillment in your life.

7. Spiritual Connection

Nurturing your spiritual well-being can provide a sense of purpose, meaning, and fulfillment in life. This can take many forms, including religious practices, meditation, prayer, or connecting with nature. Cultivating a sense of spirituality can help you navigate life's challenges with greater resilience, find inner peace, and experience a deeper sense of connection with yourself and the world around you.

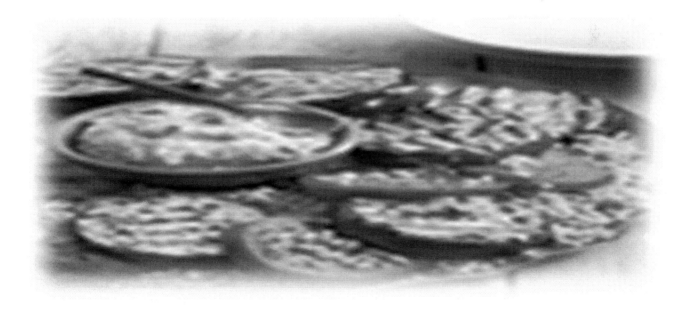

Conclusion

Thank you for joining me on this journey through the "Super Easy Keto Mediterranean Diet Cookbook for Senior" This book is more than just a collection of recipes; it's a guide to embracing a healthier, more vibrant lifestyle. By combining the principles of the ketogenic and Mediterranean diets, this book aims to help you achieve better health, maintain a healthy weight, and enjoy delicious meals that are both nutritious and satisfying.

The chapters in this book flow seamlessly from understanding the basics of these powerful diets to providing practical advice on meal planning, shopping, and cooking. Each recipe is crafted with care, considering the unique nutritional needs of seniors. With detailed instructions, nutritional values, and health benefits, every dish is designed to support your journey towards better health and wellness.

As you explore these recipes and integrate them into your daily routine, I hope you find joy in cooking and eating wholesome, flavourful meals. My writing style throughout the book is straightforward and engaging, making it easy for you to follow along and get the most out of each section. Whether you are a seasoned cook or new to the kitchen, this book is designed to be user-friendly and accessible.

I wish you the best of luck on your journey to improved health and vitality. Your feedback is incredibly valuable to me. If you have any thoughts, suggestions, or experiences you'd like to share, please let me know. Your insights will not only help me improve future editions of this book but also guide others who are considering making a positive change in their lives.

Thank you for being a part of this journey. Enjoy the delicious recipes, embrace the holistic wellness practices, and thrive in your golden years with confidence and joy.

I hope you found the dishes and advice useful and pleasant. Before you depart, I'd like to recommend two additional books that will help you on your wellness path.

Discover the "DASH Diet Mediterranean Weight Loss Solution".

Take your health to the next level with the DASH Diet Mediterranean Weight Loss Solution. This book combines the benefits of the DASH and Mediterranean diets, providing:

- Balanced, nutrient-dense recipes are ideal for heart health and long-term weight loss.
- Strategies for reducing salt and increasing nutrient-dense meals.

Adopt the "Sugar Elimination Diet for Beginners"

Consider lowering your sugar intake with the Sugar Elimination Diet for Beginners. This book provides:

- Beginner-Friendly Recipes: Simple meals to help control sugar cravings.
- Practical Advice: Methods for detecting and removing hidden sugars.

Why Do These Books Matter?

Both volumes are intended to supplement your road to greater health, offering:

- Holistic health is a balanced approach to diet.
- Diverse Recipes: More tasty, health-promoting meals.
- Sustainable Changes: Long-term practices that increase well-being.

I urge you to use these tools as you continue your road to a better, happier self. Your dedication to improved health is admirable, and these books will help you every step of the way.

To get these books are very simple, just follow the easy steps in the next page:

Kindly bring out your phone and:

1. Locate the QR of the required book

2. Open your smartphone QR scanner

3. Wait a little, notification will appear on your screen with a link or prompt

4. Tap the notification or link that appears

5. Follow the on-screen instruction to navigate

For more book like this:

Share Your Thoughts

Thank you for joining me on this journey through the "Keto Mediterranean Diet Cookbook for Seniors." Your feedback is invaluable and helps others make informed decisions.

Please take a moment to share your thoughts and experiences with this book. Your opinion helps us improve and allows others to benefit from your insights.

What did you enjoy the most?

How have the recipes and tips helped you?

Are there areas where we can improve?

Your feedback can make a difference. Thank you for your time and support!

Made in United States
Orlando, FL
16 December 2024

55690768R00074